# WISDOM *for the* Good Life

# Wisdom for the Good Life

Edward F. Grant

iUniverse, Inc.
Bloomington

**WISDOM FOR THE GOOD LIFE**



*iUniverse books may be ordered through booksellers or by contacting:*

*iUniverse*
*1663 Liberty Drive*
*Bloomington, IN 47403*
*www.iuniverse.com*
*1-800-Authors (1-800-288-4677)*



*ISBN: 978-1-4502-9309-9 (pbk)*
*ISBN: 978-1-4620-4149-7 (clth)*
*ISBN: 978-1-4502-9310-5 (ebk)*

*Printed in the United States of America*

*iUniverse rev. date: 08/10/2011*

# Contents

# Introduction

The Wisdom Books of the Bible are a marvelous treasure of priceless gems of practical wisdom for living the good life—good in terms of one's personal well-being, one's relationship with others and, to be sure, one's relationship with God. They are an important, even necessary, moral and spiritual guide for one's journey of life if, in fact, that journey strives toward the destination of realizing one's highest potential for good in one's family, one's work, one's community, one's country and in the world.

The Old Testament books of the Bible usually classified as the Wisdom Books are Job, Psalms, Proverbs, Ecclesiastes and the Song of Songs. Even though the primary message of the Song of Songs is not wisdom in the literal sense of the word, it qualifies for inclusion in this wisdom category of biblical books because its theme, while not about the love of wisdom is, so to speak, very much about the wisdom of love.

Proverbs summarizes well the purpose of biblical wisdom literature in these words:

> "Their purpose is to teach people
> wisdom and discipline, to help them
> understand the insights of the wise.
> Their purpose is to teach people
> to live disciplined and successful lives,
> to help them do what is right, just and fair."
> (Prov. 1:2-3)

According to biblical tradition, the Psalms were written by David, King of Israel(1000—962 B.C.) and Proverbs, Ecclesiastes and Song of Songs were written by David's son, Solomon who succeeded his father as King of Israel(962—922 B.C.), and whose name is synonymous with wisdom. While biblical scholarship does not agree with this tradition in its entirety, it is certainly true that many, if not most, of the Psalms were written by David. It is also quite possible, even highly probable, that some of Solomon's superior wisdom is found in parts of the three books that credit him with authorship, but conclusive proof is wanting. Evidence in some sections of these books—Proverbs, Ecclesiastes, Song of Songs—clearly point to a much later date of writing than Solomon's time.

Thus these books as we have them in the Bible, including Psalms, are a compilation from a variety of different wisdom sources and were most likely written about 400—300 B.C. Job is no doubt the work of one author and it was written about 500 B.C.

The Bible reveals that Solomon at the beginning of his reign was uniquely blessed by God, on his request, with the special gift of wisdom and in consequence achieved immense fame in Israel and around the world for the excellence of his wise words and deeds. The Queen of Sheba who visited Solomon to experience first hand the greatness of his wisdom, declared with deep conviction at the end of her visit:

> "Everything I heard in my country
> about your achievements and wisdom
> is true! I didn't believe what was said
> until I arrived here and saw it with
> my own eyes. In fact, I had not heard
> the half of it! Your wisdom and
> prosperity are far beyond what I was told."
> (1 Kings 10:6-7)

Indeed, according to the Bible, Solomon was in fact a prolific writer of proverbs and songs:

> "His fame spread throughout all the
> surrounding nations. He composed some
> 3,000 proverbs and wrote 1,005 songs.
> He could speak with authority about all
> kinds of plants, from the great cedar
> of Lebanon to the tiny hyssop that grows
> from cracks in a wall. He could also speak
> about animals, birds, small creatures and fish.
> And kings from every nation
> sent their ambassadors to listen
> to the wisdom of Solomon."
> (1 Kings 4:31-34)

This perhaps is the most important reason why the Song of Songs was numbered among the Wisdom Books. Any association of authorship with the wisest of the wise would certainly guarantee that.

But though written some 2500 years ago, the inspired principles of wisdom from the Wisdom Books, in terms of their moral and spiritual worth and value for humanity, are for any and every age and time. These timeless truths and moral insights are as relevant for us today as they were for the people and time when they were written. This, to be sure, is an important reminder—as if indeed one were needed—that their relevance for us is because, basically and fundamentally, human nature is still the same. Despite the incredible and breathtaking changes that have occurred over countless millennia in virtually every area of human endeavor, human nature has not changed from the beginning of time. The classic and endless moral struggle between good and evil within and around us as we strive to overcome evil with good, is as real for us today as it was for those who lived in the ancient past. Their wisdom, therefore, should be an indispensable moral guide for us in our quest to live the good life in an evil world.

What is the wisdom of the Wisdom Books?

What inspired and inspiring wisdom do the writers share in these books?

The fact that it is relevant for the moral struggles we encounter in our everyday lives is a clear indication that it is not wisdom of the metaphysical or abstract variety that only those of a philosophical turn of mind can figure out or understand. The wisdom of the Wisdom Books is the practical wisdom that has to do with the common issues of everyday life that all people experience and struggle with from time to time, regardless of culture, race or nationality. In other words, it is wisdom that speaks to the practical issues of our common humanity.

On the matter of love, for instance, the wisdom from Proverbs and Song of Songs, is:

"Love prospers when a fault is forgiven,
but dwelling on it
separates close friends."
(Prov. 17:9)

"Many waters cannot quench love,
nor can rivers drown it.
If a man tried to buy love
with all his wealth,
his offer would be utterly scorned."
(Song 8:7)

On anger, Psalms and Proverbs have this to say:

"Don't sin by letting anger control you.
Think about it overnight
and remain silent."
(Psalm 4:4)

"A gentle answer deflects anger,
but harsh words make tempers flare."
(Prov. 15:1)

Ecclesiastes has some insight on hard times:

> "People can never predict
> when hard times might come.
> Like fish in a net or birds in a trap,
> people are caught by sudden tragedy."
> (Eccles. 9:12)

And Job, in his reflection on humanity as a whole, makes this observation:

> "How frail is humanity!
> How short is life, and full of trouble."
> (Job 14:1)

This book, therefore, gives the wisdom of the Wisdom Books of Job, Psalms, Proverbs, Ecclesiastes, Song of Songs on a number of themes and topics that are relevant for us today, in the hope that it will be a helpful moral guide to those on the challenging journey for the good life. But the good life, to be really good, cannot be good only for oneself but has to be good also for others, for, morally speaking, a good life that is only good for oneself is not truly a good life.

Then, as the wisdom writers understand it, the good life is not a trouble-free life. Indeed, for them, such a life on the human level does not exist, and so it is pointless to strive for the trouble-free life as the moral ideal for the good life. Job expresses this point well in the above quotation.

The reason why the trouble-free life, as they see it, is not realistic or attainable is inherent in the human condition. Human beings are by nature imperfect and therefore as a result of our moral imperfection we cannot realize the perfect state of a trouble-free life. The good life then is a life that accepts troubles and struggles as a normal part of our human existence and strives to use these challenges in one's life as opportunities for one's good as well as the good of others.

The wisdom writers however acknowledge that to cope successfully and triumphantly with these challenges or troubles and to use them to the best advantage we need divine help. Our imperfection results from our sinful nature, a nature that is more prone to evil than to good. We cannot therefore always know what is the good or best course of action to take in some of life's difficult situations that we encounter from time to time.

God, in his perfection and infinite wisdom, power and goodness is the only one who can enable us to realize our potential for good in such circumstances. In other words, only God can help us turn our troubles into triumphs. In the words of Proverbs:

> "Trust in the Lord with all your heart;
> do not depend on your own understanding.
> Seek his will in all you do,
> and he will show you which path to take."
> (Prov. 3:5-6)

This book is in two parts.

The first part( Chapters 1—3 ) examines the wisdom writers' understanding of God since, in their view, he plays such a prominent and pivotal role in one's realization of the good life.

The second part( Chapters 4—26 ) gives the words of wisdom from the wisdom writers on a variety of themes and topics that are very crucial and central in one's pursuit of the good life. These themes and topics are organized in alphabetical order, hence the chapter titles are given the letters A, B, C, etc., indicating that all themes beginning with that particular letter are listed thereunder. To find, for example, what the wisdom writers have to say on "Discipline" one would go to Chapter 7 ( D ).

When there are two or more topics in the same quotation, the quotation is usually given under each topic. The following quotation is a case in point:

> "If you listen to constructive criticism,
> you will be at home among the wise."
> (Prov. 15:31)

This quotation is found under both "criticism" and "wise."

In listing the wisdom writers under each topic, the biblical order of the Wisdom Books is followed: Job, Psalms, Proverbs, Ecclesiastes, Song of Songs.

# Chapter 1

## GOD AND THE GOOD LIFE

Voltaire, the eighteenth-century French philosopher, made the insightful observation that if God did not exist, it would be necessary to invent him. The wisdom writers of the Bible would most certainly and absolutely agree. Indeed, David in the Psalms, in essence, expressed this conviction when he said that only a fool would deny the existence of God:

> "Only fools say in their hearts,
> 'There is no God.'
> They are corrupt,
> and their actions are evil;
> not one of them does good."
> (Psalms 14:1;53:1)

But while they shared a firm and abiding belief in God, they struggled time and again to have a clear and consistent understanding of this God in whom they fervently believed. They found to their utter dismay, even at times deep disappointment, that in some respects God was difficult to know and more difficult to figure out. He seemed to them at such times to be unavailable, somewhat uncaring and rather distant at the very time that they most needed him:

"If only I knew where to find God,
I would go to his court.
I go east but he is not there.
I go west but I cannot find him.
I do not see him in the north,
for he is hidden.
I look to the south,
but he is concealed."
(Job 23:3, 8-9)

"O Lord, why do you stand so far away?
Why do you hide when I am in trouble?"
(Psalm 10:1)

The wisdom writers, however, begin at the beginning and that beginning is to acknowledge God as the infinite source of all true wisdom.

Since all true wisdom begins with God and is centered in him, it is wise and necessary, therefore, first things first, that we come to God for the wisdom we need to live the good life:

"Fear of the Lord
is the foundation of true wisdom.
(Or, in the words of the NRSV:
'Fear of the Lord
is the beginning of wisdom.')
All who obey his commandments
will grow in wisdom."
(Psalm 111:10)

"The fear of the Lord is true wisdom;
to forsake evil is real understanding."
(Job 28:28)

"Fear of the Lord
is the foundation of true knowledge,
but fools despise wisdom and discipline."
(Prov. 1:7)

"Fear of the Lord
is the foundation of wisdom
Knowledge of the Holy One
results in good judgment."
(Prov.9:10)

"Fear of the Lord
is a life-giving fountain;
it offers escape from the snares of death."
(Prov. 14:27)

"Fear of the Lord leads to life,
bringing security
and protection from harm."
(Prov. 19:23)

It should be noted that "Fear of the Lord" in this context does not mean to be afraid of God in the sense of to be scared of him but rather to know him with a deep sense of awe and reverence in recognition of his infinite greatness and power.

We need God because there is so little in life in general and in our own lives in particular that we actually do control. In fact, it is precisely because so much of life is beyond our control that we encounter troubles of one kind or another all along our journey of life. In the words of Job:

"People are born for trouble,
as readily as sparks fly up from a fire."
( Job 5:7)

Indeed, in terms of the most important decision about our lives, the decision whether or not to come into this world, we had no say in the matter at all! The decision of our birth, for good or ill, was made for us by Mom and Dad, and not even with our permission! From a moral standpoint, however seemingly unjust the natural reality of birth is, from our perspective, in that the choice was not ours, the point is that it is a fact of life beyond our control. For the wisdom writers, this is certainly not a chance happening but part of the natural order of things divinely ordained by God and therefore not subject to human change or control. In the words of Ecclesiastes:

> "And I know that whatever God does
> is final. Nothing can be added to it
> or taken from it. God's purpose is
> that people should fear him."
> ( Eccles. 3:14)

The author of Ecclesiastes reminds us too that it is not only our coming into this world but also our leaving it that is completely beyond our control. Having come into this world by divine will, it is not up to us to decide whether or not to leave it. That decision has already been made for us. Death is the universal means decreed by God by which all humanity, without exception, leaves this world and there is nothing anyone can do to alter, amend or annul this divine order:

> "None of us can hold back our spirit
> from departing. None of us has the
> power to prevent the day of our death.
> There is no escaping that obligation,
> that dark battle."
> (Eccles. 8:8)

> "No one can live forever;
> all will die.
> No one can escape
> the power of the grave."
> (Psalm 89:48)

The fact that many of the crucial areas of our lives are not completely within our control is also the reason why there is so much fear in our lives.

Fear makes its unwelcome and unsettling appearance most often in such experiences as a serious illness, a tragic accident, loss of a job, a sudden financial crisis, foreclosure on one's home or some other family tragedy.

When we realize that calamity of one kind or another has struck or is about to strike and we lack the ability and or resources to cope, the experience cripples us with fear. Needless to say, fear is the bitter enemy of the good life. Fear is fiercely hostile to the good life because it robs us of real happiness and happiness is an indispensable ingredient of the good life.

In other words, it is impossible to experience the good life if one is constantly and consistently unhappy. Because work, with the many positive challenges it often brings, plays such a central role in all our lives, the author of Ecclesiastes believes that it is important to be happy in our work if we are to truly realize the good life:

> "So I saw that there is nothing
> better for people than to be happy
> in their work.
> That is why we are here!
> No one will bring us back from death
> to enjoy life after we die."
> (Eccles. 3:22)

> "So I concluded there is nothing
> better than to be happy and enjoy
> ourselves as long as we can.
> And people should eat and drink
> and enjoy the fruits of their labor,
> for these are gifts from God."
> (Eccles. 3:12-13)

And to experience that happiness in our work, it is necessary to do it well:

"Whatever you do, do well.
For when you go to the grave
there will be no work,
or planning or knowledge or wisdom."
(Eccles. 9:10)

Of course, the job that pays the best may not necessarily be the job that gives true happiness. Money, therefore, should not be the only or even the primary consideration in taking a job, if we are in pursuit of the good life, for as the author of Ecclesiastes reminds us, money can never guarantee happiness. And, most often, to be unhappy in work is to be unhappy in life:

"Those who love money
will never have enough.
How meaningless to think
that wealth brings true happiness.
The more you have,
the more people come
to help you spend it.
So what good is wealth—
except perhaps to watch it slip
through your fingers."
(Eccles. 5:10-11)

Then Proverbs rightly warns us that when our primary or exclusive pursuit of money becomes so obsessive that it degenerates to the point of greed, the inevitable result is a failure to realize the good life we earnestly seek and desire:

"Such is the fate of all
who are greedy for money;
it robs them of life."
(Prov. 1:19)

To be sure, the wisdom writers are not saying that it is wrong to have money. Indeed, they certainly recognize that money is a necessity and all of us need to have it. But it is when our desire for money is driven exclusively by greed and money becomes not a means towards the good life, but our one and only consuming passion and preoccupation, the be-all and the end-all of our lives, that it destroys the innate sense of goodness within us and thus prevents us from realizing our highest potential for good for ourselves and others. For money to fulfill its proper place in life, one needs wisdom to guide us in terms of its use, as these wisdom writers point out:

> "Wisdom is even better
> when you have money.
> Both are a benefit as you
> go through life.
> Wisdom and money can get you
> almost anything, but only wisdom
> can save your life."
> (Eccles. 7:11-12)

> "Don't wear yourself out
> trying to get rich;
> be wise enough
> to know when to quit.
> In the blink of an eye
> wealth disappears;
> for it will sprout wings
> and fly away like an eagle."
> (Prov. 23:4-5)

> "And if your wealth increases,
> don't make it the center of your life."
> (Psalm 62:10)

The point of emphasis here clearly is that there are deeper virtues and values in life than money that contribute to our true happiness within.

Money can certainly provide us with the material things to satisfy our physical needs and selfish desires. But, needless to say, in the view of the wisdom writers, it is folly to think that the more material possessions we acquire is the happier we will be.

To be rich is not evil in and of itself. What is evil are the means and methods often used to become wealthy. This is why money should not be one's primary or exclusive goal in life, for when it is, one is likely to resort to any and all means, however extreme or evil, to achieve this goal and in the process corrupt or ruin one's personal life as well as, at times, the lives of others. If this is what it costs to be rich then, for the wisdom writers, it is too high a price to pay. One's personal integrity is too priceless:

"Better to be godly and have little
than to be evil and rich.
For the strength of the wicked
will be shattered,
but the Lord takes care of the godly."
(Psalm 37:16-17)

"Evil people get rich for the moment,
but the reward of the godly will last!"
(Prov. 11:18)

"Better to have little with godliness
than to be rich and dishonest."
(Prov. 16:8)

"Better to be poor and honest
than to be dishonest and rich."
(Prov. 28:6)

"The trustworthy person
will get a rich reward,
but a person who wants quick riches
will get into trouble."
(Prov. 28:30)

If we are fortunate to be blessed with wealth and that wealth is honestly acquired through hard work and wise and prudent investments, we should regard such wealth as a gift from God. Since it is a gift from God, a sure way to increase it is not by selfishly hoarding it to lavishly spend it all on oneself, but by sharing it joyfully with others. When we give generously to those in need, God in turn rewards our generosity with bountiful blessings:

> "Give freely and become more wealthy;
> be stingy and lose everything."
> (Prov. 11:24)

> "The blessing of the Lord
> makes a person rich,
> and he adds no sorrow with it."
> (Prov. 10:22)

> "If you help the poor
> you are lending to the Lord—
> and he will repay you."
> (Prov. 19:17)

The wise course to pursue in terms of money, according to Proverbs, is to seek "neither poverty nor riches":

> "O God, I beg two favors from you:
> let me have them before I die.
> First, help me never to tell a lie.
> Second, give me neither poverty nor riches!
> Give me just enough
> to satisfy my needs.
> For if I grow rich,
> I may deny you and say,
> 'Who is the Lord?'
> And if I am too poor,
> I may steal and thus
> insult God's holy name."
> (Prov. 30:7-9)

Since, for the wisdom writers, the good life cannot, and indeed must not, be based on the uncertainty of material wealth, which may be here today but also may be gone tomorrow, one must of necessity anchor the good life in God, for because he is perfectly wise, just and good he alone can guarantee us true fulfillment and happiness in our lives and also make us instruments of peace, hope and love to others.

As we have already observed, for these inspired wisdom writers the existence of God is so clearly and readily obvious that David found it necessary to say that only a fool would deny God's existence. David thought, too, that the world of nature is an eloquent expression and a marvelous demonstration of God at work:

> "When I look at the night sky
> and see the work of your fingers—
> the moon and the stars
> you set in place—
> what are mere mortals that
> you should think about them,
> human beings that
> you should care for them."
> (Psalm 8:3-4)

> "The heavens proclaim the glory of God.
> The skies display his craftsmanship.
> Day after day they continue to speak;
> night after night
> they make him known.
> They speak without a sound or word;
> their voice is never heard.
> Yet their message has gone
> throughout the earth,
> and their words to all the world.
> God has made a home
> in the heavens for the sun.
> It bursts forth like a radiant bridegroom
> after his wedding.

It rejoices like a great athlete
eager to run the race.
The sun rises at one end of the heavens
and follows its course to the other end.
Nothing can hide from its heat."
(Psalm 19:1-6)

In the book of Job, God speaks to Job from the whirlwind in terms of his role as Creator:

"Then the Lord answered Job
from the whirlwind:
'Who is this that questions my wisdom
with such ignorant words?
Brace yourself like a man,
because I have some questions for you,
and you must answer them.
Where were you when I laid
the foundations of the earth?
Tell me, if you know so much.
Who determined its dimensions
and stretched out the surveying line?
Who supports its foundations,
and who laid its cornerstone
as the morning stars sang together
and all the angels shouted for joy?
Who kept the sea inside its boundaries,
as it burst from the womb,
and as I clothed it with clouds,
and wrapped it in thick darkness?
For I locked it behind barrel gates,
limiting its shores.
I said, 'This far and no farther
will you come.
Here your proud waves must stop!'"
(Job 38:1-11)

God's divine imprint is not only inscribed on all areas and aspects of the natural world but is even more impressive and convincing in his creation of humanity, created as we are in his own image and given authority over his whole creation:

> "Yet you made them (human beings)
> only a little lower than God and
> crowned them with glory and honor.
> You gave them charge of everything
> you made, putting all things
> under their authority—
> the flocks and the herds,
> and all the wild animals,
> the birds in the sky,
> the fish in the sea
> and everything that swims
> the ocean currents.
> O Lord, our Lord,
> your majestic name fills the earth!"
> (Psalm 8:5-9)

Job acknowledges the divine imprint on his own personal life from the very moment of conception:

> "You guided my conception
> and formed me in the womb.
> You clothed me with skin and flesh
> and you knit my bones
> and sinews together.
> You gave me life
> and showed me your unfailing love.
> My life was preserved by your care."
> (Job 10:10-12)

For the author of Ecclesiastes, human conception is a divine mystery beyond our finite and limited understanding:

"Just as you cannot understand
the path of the wind
or the mystery of a tiny baby
growing in its mother's womb,
so you cannot understand
the activity of God, who does all things."
(Eccles. 11:5)

David in Psalm 139 is in absolute awe of the marvelous and intricate system by which the human body, with all its diverse parts, functions so efficiently and effectively. This to him is clearly and beyond any doubt the mysterious and creative hand of God at work:

"You made all the delicate,
inner parts of my body
and knit me together
in my mother's womb.
Thank you for making me
so wonderfully complete!
Your workmanship is marvelous—
how well I know it.
You watched me
as I was being formed
in utter seclusion,
as I was woven together
in the dark of the womb.
You saw me before I was born.
Every day of my life
was recorded in your book.
Every moment was laid out
before a single day had passed."
(Psalm 139:13-16)

This mystery in terms of God's creation as a whole and his creation of humanity in particular, though it utterly defies human comprehension, is to the wisdom writers, somewhat understandable for we were created in God's image as the Genesis account of creation tells us:

> "So God created human beings
> in his own image.
> In the image of God
> he created them;
> male and female he created them."
> (Gen. 1:27)

Since God himself is the mystery of mysteries, his creation of humanity in his image is no less a mystery.

Humanity, in the thinking of the wisdom writers, was originally created good, for God being perfectly good would not create that which is evil, particularly if that creation is in his own image. But though created good, humanity was created with the potential for evil. In other words, humanity was given the right of free choice, for that is what, among other things, is meant by being created in God's image. Humanity could therefore either choose to pursue the path of the good in life and thus be an instrument for good to others, or pursue the path of evil in life with tragic and evil consequences for others. This then indicates humanity's moral imperfection, for though created good, we were not created perfectly good. Only God is perfectly good. That is to say, regardless of what heights of moral goodness the best among us may be able to aspire to and realize, none of us possess the ability to always do what is right and good. In the words of Ecclesiastes:

> "Not a single person on earth
> is always good and never sins."
> (Eccles. 7:20)

Psalm 14 makes basically the same point:

> "The Lord looks down from heaven
> on the entire human race;
> he looks to see if anyone is truly wise,

if anyone seeks God.
But no, all have turned away;
all have become corrupt.
No one does good, not a single one!"
(Psalm 14:2-3)

And Proverbs asks rhetorically:

"Who can say,
'I have cleansed my heart:
I am pure and free from sin?'"
(Prov. 20:9)

We realize the nature of our moral imperfection all too clearly, in particular as we struggle against the forces of evil in our lives, a struggle in which we are all constantly and continuously engaged. It's an experience that at times reveals our moral weakness and the subtle power of evil.

The moral battlefield within, the scene of bitter warfare between the forces of good and evil, is the human heart. The battles that are fought there are the most important battles we will ever have to fight and thus their consequences, needless to say, have the power to determine the nature and quality of our lives in terms of whether or not the good life is a realistic option for us. So the author of Proverbs rightly warns us to guard this moral center of our lives with the utmost diligence, because failure to do so could mean sad ruin for our lives:

"Guard your heart above all else,
for it determines
the course of your life."
(Prov. 4:23)

To be sure, it is the right motives from our hearts coupled with how well we are able to overcome evil with good in consistent action, that will reveal our true moral worth and determine the kind of impact we make on others, on our community and in the world.

David, in the Psalms, realizing the power of one's motives and driven by his deep desire and yearning to do the right and the good, prays for God to examine his heart and motives to ensure that he is on the right track for the good and well-being of his people and nation:

"Declare me innocent, O Lord,
for I have acted with integrity;
I have trusted in the Lord
without wavering.
Put me on trial, Lord,
and cross examine me.
Test my motives and my heart."
(Psalm 26:1-2)

"Search me, O God, and know my heart;
test me and know my anxious thoughts.
Point out anything in me
that offends you,
and lead me along the path
of everlasting life."
(Psalm 139:23-24)

In terms of this moral civil war within us between good and evil, right and wrong, that we struggle with all through our lives, the wisdom writers warn us about underestimating the power of evil, a warning that is necessary even for those who think that they are morally mature and strong.

Indeed, David himself is a classic case in point. Even though he was a man of deep, passionate faith and possessed a high moral sense of virtue and integrity, David succumbed to the powerful evils of adultery and murder.

He happened to be on the roof of his palace one day when David saw Bathsheba taking a bath. Bathsheba was the wife of Uriah the Hittite, who was a member of David's elite military force, The Thirty Mighty Men.

Attracted by her physical beauty and overcome with a lustful desire for a sexual relationship with her, David sent for her and satisfied his sexual passion in an adulterous affair with her. Bathsheba subsequently informed David that she was pregnant. David then arranged with Joab, Commander of his army, for her husband, Uriah, to be in the frontline of the battle that Israel was fighting against the Philistines. Uriah, as David hoped, was killed in that battle. David then took Bathsheba as one of his wives. When David was confronted by the prophet, Nathan, with his sinful behavior in terms of both Bathsheba and Uriah, in deep repentance and remorse, he prayed for God's forgiveness:

> "Have mercy on me, O God,
> because of your unfailing love.
> Because of your great compassion,
> blot out the stain of my sins.
> Wash me clean from my guilt.
> Purify me from my sin.
> For I recognize my rebellion;
> it haunts me day and night.
> Against you, and you alone,
> have I sinned;
> I have done what is evil in your sight.
> You will be proved right
> in what you say,
> and your judgment against me is just.
> For I was born a sinner—
> yes, from the moment
> my mother conceived me.
> But you desire honesty from the womb,
> teaching me wisdom there.
> Purify me from my sins,
> and I will be clean;
> wash me and I will be whiter than snow.
> Oh, give me back my joy again;
> you have broken me—
> now let me rejoice.
> Don't keep looking at my sins.
> Remove the stain of my guilt.
> Create in me a clean heart, O God
> Renew a loyal spirit within me."
> (Psalm 51:1-10)

To be sure, it is not that David did not know that adultery is a sin. Psalm 51 is not only a clear admission of guilt but also expresses the depth of his remorse as he seeks God's forgiveness. It is, rather, a convincing example of the power of evil within the human heart, over which at times we seem to have little or no control, even after we have done our best to overcome it.

The sin or evil that overpowers us from within, particularly at times when we are most vulnerable, may not be adultery, as in David's case, or any other sexual sin. But whatever it is, be it lying or stealing, envy or jealousy, hate or violence, greed or graft, bribery or deceit, abuse of one kind or another, etc., etc., the point is that the moment of surrender to some sin(s) that seems to control us, comes to each of us at one time or another.

Jesus confirms that the true source of all these sins is the heart:

> "And then he added:
> 'It is what comes from inside
> that defiles you.
> For from within, out of a person's heart,
> come evil thoughts, sexual immorality,
> theft, murder, adultery, greed,
> lustful desires, envy,
> slander, pride and foolishness.
> All these vile things come from within;
> they are what defile you.'"
> (Mark 7:20-23)

If we do not control the sins in our own lives, needless to say, they will control us:

> "How can I know all the sins
> lurking in my heart?
> Cleanse me from these hidden faults.
> Keep your servant from deliberate sins.
> Don't let them control me.

Then I will be free of guilt
and innocent of great sin.
May the words of my mouth
and the meditation of my heart
be pleasing to you,
O Lord, my rock and my redeemer."
(Psalm 19:12-14)

The author of Proverbs 5 also reminds us of the power that evil can have over us:

"An evil man is held captive
by his own sins;
they are ropes that catch and hold him.
He will die for lack of self-control;
he will be lost
because of his great foolishness."
(Prov. 5:22-23)

Then Ecclesiastes emphasizes that when we strive for perfection in wisdom, this can really be a fruitless exercise:

"I have always tried my best
to let wisdom guide my thoughts
and actions. I said to myself:
'I am determined to be wise.'
But it didn't work.
Wisdom is always distant
and difficult to find.
I searched everywhere,
determined to find wisdom
and to understand the reason for things.
I was determined to prove to myself
that wickedness is stupid
and that foolishness is madness."
(Eccles. 7:23-25)

Paul in the New Testament addresses this same issue of the moral struggle against evil within one's heart in his letter to Christians in Rome.

It would seem that Paul found it necessary to clarify this issue for first generation Christians so that they would not be under any misunderstanding

that now that they were Christians, the moral conflict within between good and evil, right and wrong, would be a thing of the past. The point here is that they should not belittle or underestimate the power of evil, even in a Christian heart. And, as if to make his case much stronger, Paul presents it not in general terms but in a deeply personal way:

> "So the trouble is not with the law,
> for it is spiritual and good.
> The trouble is with me,
> for I am all too human, a slave to sin.
> I don't really understand myself,
> for I want to do what is right,
> but I don't do it.
> Instead, I do what I hate.
> But if I know that what I am doing is wrong,
> this shows that I agree that the law is good.
> So I am not the one doing the wrong;
> it is sin living in me that does it.
> And I know that nothing good lives in me,
> that is, in my sinful nature.
> I want to do what is right, but I can't.
> I want to do what is good, but I don't.
> I don't want to do what is wrong,
> but I do it anyway.
> But if I do what I don't want to do,
> I am not really the one doing it;
> it is sin living in me that does it.
> I have discovered this principle of life—
> that when I want to do what is right,
> I inevitably do what is wrong.
> I love God's law with all my heart.

> But there is another power within me
> that is at war with my mind.
> This power makes me a slave
> to the sin that is still within me.
> Oh, what a miserable person I am!
> Who will free me from this life
> that is dominated by sin and death?
> Thank God!
> The answer is in Jesus Christ our Lord.
> So you see how it is:
> In my mind,
> I really want to obey God's law,
> but because of my sinful nature
> I am a slave to sin."
> (Rom. 7:14-25)

Paul's answer to his personal moral dilemma—"that when I want to do what is right, I inevitably do what is wrong"—is similar to David's.

In a word, the answer is: God!

In Paul's case, in Christian terms, "the answer is Jesus Christ our Lord."

David's prayer in Psalm 19 is a recognition that he is powerless on his own to control sin in his inner life. He therefore concludes that only God can give him the power to conquer evil from within. Thus his prayer is in fact an appeal for divine help:

> "Keep your servant from deliberate sins!
> Don't let them control me.
> Then I will be free of guilt
> and innocent of great sin."
> (Psalm 19:13)

For the wisdom writers therefore, David in particular, the resolution of this moral conflict within in the triumph of good over evil, right over wrong, is not possible without God. This then, morally speaking, is a powerful and convincing argument for the existence of God, for their firm belief is that apart from God, the infinite source of all good, doing the right and the good would be virtually impossible, given humanity's imperfect, sinful nature.

But while these inspired writers of Old Testament wisdom are absolutely convinced of God's existence, they readily acknowledge that God is a mystery to the human mind. Indeed, if he is truly God it goes without saying that by virtue of his divine nature, he has to be completely beyond human comprehension. Imperfect humanity, conditioned by space and time, can never accurately conceive, let alone fully understand a perfect God, whose perfection means, among other things, that he is both eternal and omnipotent. If we could understand God in all his mysterious, infinite greatness and power, then, to be sure, God would not be God.

Thus, for the wisdom writers, the first principle of true human wisdom is to recognize that God and his works are a divine mystery, totally beyond the reach of our finite understanding and mental abilities. In the book of Job Zophar, in his questions to Job, reminds him that our limited understanding does not permit us to know all there is to know about God:

> "Can you solve the mysteries of God?
> Can you discover everything
> about the Almighty?
> Such knowledge is higher than the heavens—
> and who are you?
> It is deeper than the underworld—
> what do you know?
> It is broader than the earth
> and wider than the sea."
> (Job 11:7-9)

And Job acknowledges that God's power is beyond human comprehension:

> "God stretches the northern sky
> over empty space and
> hangs the earth on nothing.
> He wraps the rain in his thick clouds,

and the clouds
don't burst with the weight.
He covers the face of the moon,
shrouding it with his clouds.
He created the horizon
when he separated the waters;
he set the boundary
between day and night.
The foundations of heaven tremble;
they shudder at his rebuke.
By his power the sea grew calm.
By his skill
he crushed the great sea monster.
His spirit made the heavens beautiful,
and his power
pierced the gliding serpent.
These are just the beginning
of all that he does;
merely a whisper of his power.
Who then can comprehend
the thunder of his power?"
Job 26:7-14)

The Psalms are eloquent in their praise of a God who is perfect and eternal, with no limitations on his power and greatness:

"God's way is perfect.
All the Lord's promises prove true.
He is a shield for all
who look to him for protection.
For who is God except the Lord?
Who but our God is a solid rock."
(Psalm 18:30-31)

"I will exalt you, my God and King,
and praise your name forever and ever.
I will praise you every day;
yes, I will praise you forever.
Great is the Lord!
He is most worthy of praise!
No one can measure his greatness.
Let each generation tell its children
of your mighty acts;
let them proclaim your power.
I will meditate on your majestic,
glorious splendor
and your wonderful miracles.
Your awe-inspiring deeds
will be on every tongue;
I will proclaim your greatness.
Everyone will share the story
of your wonderful greatness;
they will sing with joy
about your righteousness.
The Lord is merciful and compassionate,
slow to get angry,
and filled with unfailing love.
The Lord is good to everyone.
He showers compassion on all his creation."
(Psalm 145:1-9)

"How great is our Lord!
His power is absolute!
His understanding
is beyond comprehension!"
(Psalm 147:5)

In Proverbs the message is that God's infinite power is supreme over all human systems:

"No human wisdom or understanding
or plan can stand against the Lord!"
(Prov. 21:30)

Ecclesiastes reveals that no human mind can fully fathom the incredible works of God:

"In my search for wisdom
and in my observation
of people's burdens here on earth,
I discovered that there is
ceaseless activity, day and night.
I realized that no one can discover
everything God is doing under the sun.
Not even the wisest people discover
everything, no matter what they claim."
(Eccles. 8:16-17)

Paul also is virtually on the same page with the wisdom writers on human inability to fathom the mysterious works of God:

"Oh, how great are God's riches
and wisdom and knowledge!
How impossible it is for us to
understand his decisions and ways!
For who can know the Lord's thoughts?
Who knows enough to give him advice?
And who has given him so much
that he needs to pay it back?
For everything comes from him
and exists by his power
and is intended for his glory.
All glory to him forever! Amen."
(Rom. 11:33-36)

# Chapter 2

## THE MYSTERY OF DIVINE JUSTICE

But the mystery that is God, though completely beyond human comprehension, is, for the wisdom writers, a mystery that needs to be explored to the limits of human wisdom, for from such exploration inevitably comes spiritual growth and moral insight. And so these biblical writers are constantly and continuously engaged in a difficult struggle to understand the works and ways of God in his relationship with humanity.

In no area do they experience more difficulty, if not frustration, in figuring out the divine mind and will as in the area of God's justice. In particular, they seem to be profoundly perplexed and challenged by the classic moral and justice issue that saints and sages have wrestled with from time immemorial—why do the good suffer and the wicked prosper?

The problem, as they see it, is that if indeed God is in control of all of life, if indeed he is a perfectly good and just God, and if indeed he possesses absolute power to reward the good and punish the wicked, then why do good people suffer and wicked people prosper in the world? In the words of Job:

> "Why do the wicked prosper,
> growing old and powerful?
> They live to see their children
> grow up and settle down,
> and they enjoy their grandchildren.
> Their homes are safe from fear,
> and God does not punish them."
> (Job 21:7-9)

"Why doesn't the Almighty
bring the wicked to judgment?
Why must the godly
wait for him in vain?"
(Job 24:1)

The author of Psalm 73 wonders whether he has kept his "heart pure for nothing" because all that he seems to get for it is "trouble all day long":

"Look at these wicked people—
enjoying a life of ease
while their riches multiply.
Did I keep my heart pure for nothing?
Did I keep myself
innocent for no reason?
I get nothing but trouble all day long;
every morning brings me pain."
(Psalm 73:12-14)

Indeed, the primary purpose of the book of Job is clearly to address this very issue—why do good people suffer? Job was not just a good man—he was exceptionally good. God, in his dialogue with Satan about Job, speaks of Job as "the finest man in all the earth." (Job 1:8)

"He was blameless—
a man of complete integrity.
He feared God and
stayed away from evil.
He had seven sons and three daughters.
He owned 7000 sheep, 3000 camels,
500 teams of oxen and
500 female donkeys.
He also had many servants.
He was, in fact,
the richest person in that entire area."
(Job 1:1-3)

But all of a sudden, Job is hit by disastrous tragedy and misfortune from all sides, so sweeping in fact that before long Job had lost everything he had, including all of his children. From the lofty heights of power, prestige and wealth Job had fallen to a level of poverty, humiliation and destitution that was truly appalling. And when it seemed as if his suffering could not get any worse, he was then afflicted with a disease that left him physically emaciated and disfigured, so much so that his friends did not even recognize him when they came to comfort and console him. Lamenting the magnitude of his suffering, Job defers to the will of God:

> "I came naked from my mother's womb
> and I will be naked when I leave.
> The Lord gave me what I had
> and the Lord has taken it away.
> Praise the name of the Lord!"
> (Job 1:21)

His wife, understandably bitter over the seeming injustice of it all, tells him to: "Curse God and die." (Job 2:9) His friends Bildad, Zophar and Eliphaz stopped by to visit with him when they heard of his tragic misfortunes. They were joined later by Elihu. They came to comfort him but ended up condemning him in rather unforgiving terms. Their condemnation was grounded in the conviction of a perfectly just and fair God who unfailingly dispenses impartial justice to everyone in terms of what they truly deserve, according to their deeds. Consequently, to their thinking, God would not afflict or permit anyone to be afflicted with the calamitous tragedies Job experienced if that person was truly good. Job therefore, according to this line of theological reasoning, could not be the good person he claimed, and appeared to be. They thus inevitably, even if reluctantly, concluded that their friend Job was not the exemplary leader of highest moral virtue and social conscience that they thought he was, but was instead a very evil person. The magnitude of his suffering and misfortunes would permit them no other conclusion. For to say that Job was indeed a good person in spite of this overwhelming evidence to the contrary was, in fact, to say that God was an unjust God. Evil consequences always result from evil deeds as determined and decreed by a just God. Job, therefore, was now reaping the evil consequences of intolerable suffering because of his many evil deeds. Their advice to Job was that he needed to repent of his sins and seek God's forgiveness if he wanted to be on good terms with God and experience his bountiful blessings. Zophar, in fact, thinks that Job's sins were so great that he was actually getting off lightly from a very compassionate God:

> "You claim, 'My beliefs are pure,
> and I am clean in the sight of God.'
> If only God would speak:
> if only he would tell you
> what he thinks!
> If only he would tell you
> the secrets of wisdom,
> for true wisdom is not a simple matter.
> Listen! God is doubtless punishing you
> far less than you deserve!
> If only you would prepare your heart,
> and lift up your hands
> to him in prayer!
> Get rid of your sins,
> and leave all iniquity behind you.
> Then your face will
> brighten with innocence.
> You will be strong and free of fear.
> You will forget your misery;
> it will be like water flowing away.
> Your life will be brighter
> than the noonday.
> Even darkness will be as bright as morning."
> (Job 11:4-6, 13-17)

Totally frustrated that he has failed to convince his friends that he is not the wicked sinner they accuse him of being, Job is deeply disappointed and very angry with them for not believing him:

"Teach me and I will be quiet.
Show me what I have done wrong.
Honest words can be painful,
but what do your criticisms amount to?
Do you think your words
are convincing when you disregard
my cry of desperation?
You would even send an orphan
into slavery, or sell a friend.
Look at me!
Would I lie to your face?
Stop assuming my guilt,
for I have done no wrong.
Do you think I am lying?
Don't I know the difference
between right and wrong?"
(Job 6:24-30)

But Job is also disturbed and dumbfounded by God's apparently unfair system of justice, which seems to reward good people with suffering and tragedy and evil people with security and prosperity. He is even more baffled because God's system of justice is supposed to be the only perfect one that exists. As Job sees it, God certainly knows that he is a good person.

And Job is right, for in God's own words:

"He is the finest man in all the earth.
He is blameless—
a man of complete integrity.
He fears God
and stays away from evil."
(Job 1:8)

God therefore knows that the evil accusations of Job's friends against him are false. But by permitting Job to be afflicted with the many calamities and suffering he has experienced, God is making the argument of Job 's friends seem rather convincing, because in a fair system of justice it is indeed evil people who are punished for their misdeeds and good people who are favorably rewarded for their good deeds. Job therefore wants God to explain exactly what is going on in the divine world of perfect justice, as it relates to Job and his multitude of tragedies. He thinks he is entitled to an explanation, because he has always conscientiously tried to be the best person he could possibly be, by doing what is just, right and good for his fellow men and women:

> "O God, grant me these two things,
> and then I will be able to face you.
> Remove your heavy hand from me,
> and don't terrify me
> with your awesome presence.
> Now summon me, and I will answer!
> Or let me speak to you, and you reply.
> Tell me, what have I done wrong?
> Show me my rebellion and my sin.
> Why do you turn away from me?
> Why do you treat me as your enemy?"
> (Job 13:20-24)

> "You must defend my innocence, O God,
> since no one else will stand up for me."
> (Job 17:3)

> "My complaint is with God,
> not with people.
> I have good reason to be so impatient."
> (Job 21:4)

Job even thinks that perhaps he needs a mediator between him and God, because he does not at this point fully understand God's justice, and a mediator would more readily and sympathetically see things from Job's perspective:

"God is not a mortal like me,
so I cannot argue with him
or take him to trial.
If only there were a mediator between us,
someone who could bring us together.
The mediator could make God
stop beating me, and I would no longer
live in terror of his punishment.
Then I could speak to him without fear,
but I cannot do that
in my own strength."
(Job 9:32-35)

Job's basic complaint with God is that he cannot understand why a God who is perfectly just and fair and who certainly knows about all the criminal misdeeds of evil people, does not punish them accordingly but instead allows them to succeed and prosper in life, while good people suffer for being good. Clearly, the question that torments Job more than any other in all of this is, that if all that good people get for being good is suffering and tragedy, while evil people prosper, then what is the advantage or incentive for being good? Indeed, according to Job, evil people even mock God in their prosperity with questions like: "Who is the Almighty, and why should we obey him?"—and seem to get away with it:

"They(wicked) spend their days in prosperity,
then go down to the grave in peace.
And yet they say to God, 'Go away.
We want no part of you and your ways.
Who is the Almighty,
and why should we obey him?
What good will it do us to pray?
(They think their prosperity is of
their own doing,
but I will have nothing to do
with that kind of thinking.)
Yet the light of the wicked

never seems to be extinguished.
Do they ever have trouble?
Does God distribute sorrows
to them in anger?"
(Job 21:13-17)

"You will tell me of rich and wicked people,
whose houses have vanished
because of their sins.
But ask those who have been around;
and they will tell you the truth.
Evil people are spared
in times of calamity,
and are allowed to escape disaster."
(Job 21:28-30)

The Psalms speak in similar terms of the material prosperity of the wicked, much to the consternation and confusion of the righteous, particularly since God, the Sovereign Lord of justice, sees and knows all about their evil schemes and deeds:

"Truly God is good to Israel,
to those whose hearts are pure.
But as for me, I almost lost my footing.
My feet were slipping,
and I was almost gone.
For I envied the proud,
when I saw them prosper
despite their wickedness.
They seem to live such painless lives;
their bodies are so healthy and strong.
They don't have troubles
like other people;
they're not plagued with problems
like everyone else.
They wear pride

like a jeweled necklace
and clothe themselves with cruelty.
These fat cats have everything
their hearts could ever wish for!
They scoff and speak only evil;
in their pride
they seek to crush others.
They boast against the very heavens,
and their words
strut throughout the earth.
And so the people
are dismayed and confused,
drinking in all their words.
'What does God know?' they ask.
'Does the Most High
even know what's happening?'"
(Psalm 73:1-11)

Even in death the wicked seem to do pretty well, according to Ecclesiastes:

"I have seen wicked people
buried with honor.
Yet they were the very ones
who frequented the temple
and are now praised in the same city,
where they committed their crimes."
(Eccles. 8:10)

The author of Psalm 94 cannot understand why God is taking so long to execute judgment on the wicked and thus bring an end to their boastful gloating:

"Arise, O judge of the earth.
Give the proud what they deserve.
How long, O Lord?

How long will the wicked
be allowed to gloat?
How long will they speak with arrogance?
How long will these evil people boast?
They crush your people, Lord,
hurting those you claim as your own.
They kill widows and foreigners
and murder orphans.
'The Lord isn't looking,' they say,
'And besides, the God of Israel doesn't care.'"
(Psalm 94:2-7)

Not only do the wisdom writers have serious problems with a divine justice that seems to reward the wicked with prosperity for their evil deeds, but they are at a loss to understand God's seeming indifference to the suffering of the righteous at their hour of deepest need. God seems to be totally unavailable and very distant at the very time when they need him the most. There is complete silence from him, despite their many desperate prayers and calls to him for help. God just seems indeed not to care.

Job is angry, anxious, scared and somewhat devoid of all hope as he relentlessly seeks for God, only to discover that God is nowhere to be found:

"My complaint today is still a bitter one,
and I try hard not to groan aloud.
If only I knew where to find God,
I would go to his court.
I would lay out my case
and present my arguments.
Then I would listen to his reply
and understand what he says to me.
Would he use his great power
to argue with me?
No, he would give me a fair hearing.
Honest people can reason with him,
so I would be forever

acquitted by my judge.
I go east, but he is not there.
I go west, but I cannot find him.
I do not see him in the north,
for he is hidden.
I look to the south,
but he is concealed."
(Job 23:1-9)

"So he will do to me
whatever he has planned.
He controls my destiny.
No wonder I am so terrified
in his presence.
When I think of it, terror grips me.
God has made me sick at heart;
the Almighty has terrified me.
Darkness is all around me;
thick, impenetrable darkness is everywhere."
(Job 23:14-17)

"I cry to you, O God,
but you don't answer.
I stand before you,
but you don't even look.
You have become cruel toward me.
You use your power to persecute me.
You throw me into the whirlwind
and destroy me in the storm.
And I know
you are sending me to my death,
the destination of all who live."
(Job 30:20-23)

David, too, feels as if God has abandoned him in his hour of need. He urgently needs God's help and needs it right away, but God appears to be in no hurry to respond to his desperate appeal:

> "My God, my God,
> why have you abandoned me?
> Why are you so far away
> when I groan for help?
> Everyday I call to you, my God,
> but you do not answer.
> Every night you hear my voice,
> but I find no relief."
> (Psalm 22:1-2)
>
> "O Lord, do not stay far away!
> You are my strength;
> come quickly to my aid!
> Save me from the sword;
> spare my precious life from these dogs.
> Snatch me from the lion's jaws
> and from the horns of these wild oxen."
> (Psalm 22:19-21)
>
> "O God, whom I praise,
> don't stand silent and aloof,
> while the wicked slander me
> and tell lies about me.
> They surround me with hateful words
> and fight against me for no reason."
> (Psalm 109:1-3)

"O Lord, I am calling you.
Please hurry!
Listen when I cry to you for help!
Accept my prayer
as incense offered to you,
and my upraised hands
as an evening offering."
(Psalm 141:1-2)

"Hear my prayer, O Lord;
listen to my plea!
Answer me
because you are faithful and righteous.
Don't put your servant on trial,
for no one is innocent before you.
My enemy has chased me.
He has knocked me to the ground
and forces me to live in darkness
like those in the grave.
I am losing all hope;
I am paralyzed with fear.
Come quickly Lord, and answer me,
for my depression deepens.
Don't turn away from me, or I will die."
(Psalm 143:1-4, 7)

But in their quest to understand the perfect ways and will of God, the wisdom writers conclude that to figure out the true nature of divine justice, one needs to look at the whole picture and not just a part of it. In other words, one needs to look at it from a long-term and not just a short-term perspective. Thus, even though the apparent prosperity of the wicked seems undeniable, in reality it is a prosperity that is short-lived.It does not last. The wicked may celebrate their good fortune for a while, but in the end they will surely reap the bitter consequences of their evil deeds. And so the authors of Proverbs 24 and Psalm 37 warn that it is not wise to envy the wicked:

"Don't fret because of evildoers;
don't envy the wicked.
For evil people have no future;
the light of the wicked
will be snuffed out."
(Prov. 24:19-20)

"Don't worry about the wicked
or envy those who do wrong.
For like grass, they soon fade away.
Like spring flowers, they soon wither."
(Psalm 37:1-2)
"I have seen wicked and ruthless people,
flourishing like a tree in its native soil.
But when I looked again,
they were gone!
Though I searched for them,
I could not find them!"
(Psalm 37:35-36)

Zophar reminds Job that the fleeting triumph of the wicked is nothing new. As he sees it, this has been the case all through the history of humanity:

"Don't you realize
that from the beginning of time,
ever since people
were first placed on the earth,
the triumph of the wicked
has been short-lived,
and the joy of the godless
has been only temporary?"
(Job 20:4-5)

And Eliphaz is convinced that though the wicked are indeed prosperous, their prosperity will not last:

> "These wicked people
> are heavy and prosperous;
> their waists bulge with fat.
> But their cities will be ruined.
> They will live in abandoned houses
> that are ready to tumble down.
> Their riches will not last,
> and their wealth will not endure.
> Their possessions will no longer
> spread across the horizon."
> (Job 15:27-29)

When we look at the whole picture in terms of good people who suffer, what we find is a picture quite revealing about God's justice for those who fearlessly and faithfully strive to be good and to do good in spite of great adversity. What it clearly reveals is that God always has the last word on these exemplary lives of moral courage and inspiration, and that last word, most consistently, is neither suffering nor tragedy. On the contrary, his last word is almost always victory, vindication or redemption. But as the wisdom writers discovered, God often takes a rather long time to make his triumphant appearance—so long in fact that it sometimes drives the suffering saint to the brink of despair bordering on desperation.

Again, it is another example of the bitter moral conflict between good and evil and God guarantees that for the good who suffer, the evil of suffering would not have the last word in their lives and thus be in the position to claim victory.

In the book of Job, God finally shows up—at the very end, of course, when Job had just about given up all hope. He comes in a whirlwind and reminds Job that as Creator of the universe, all the marvelous, fearsome creatures and the mysterious wonders in the natural world are eloquent expressions of his awesome, limitless divine power. God's point to Job here obviously is that if God exercises such incredible, infinite power over the whole universe he has created and everything in it, as a just God he most certainly can be depended on to see to it that Job receives true justice for the good life he has lived. Thus, as to Job's serious concerns and questions about the true nature and fairness of God's justice, because of Job's many disastrous tragedies and calamities, God addresses the whole issue directly with this question to Job: "Will you discredit my justice and condemn me just to prove that you are right?" (Job 40:8)

God's appearance, needless to say, radically changed everything.

It was what Job was earnestly and urgently seeking all along. Job was deeply troubled because God's silence and absence from his life extended for such a long time, a time when tragic circumstances were completely beyond his control and even getting worse. This, to be sure, was the time when God was most needed. But so far as Job was concerned, God was nowhere to be found.

Job was truly remorseful after God challenged him on some of his deepest concerns:

> "I know that you can do anything,
> and no one can stop you.
> You asked, 'Who is this that questions
> my wisdom with such ignorance?'
> It is I—and I was talking about
> things I knew nothing about,
> things far too wonderful for me.
> You said, 'Listen, and I will speak!
> I have some questions for you,
> and you must answer them.'
> I had only heard about you before,
> but now I have seen you
> with my own eyes.
> I take back everything I said,
> and I sit in dust and ashes
> to show my repentance."
> (Job 42:2-6)

But God never comes empty-handed, particularly when he comes after such a long absence to declare victory of good over evil in the life of "the finest man in all the earth." (Job 1:8) God's last word in fact was his triumphant deed of vindication on Job's behalf. He brought with him a blessing that triumphantly and eloquently expressed the victory of good over evil in Job's life. Job's friends were angrily rebuked by God for their accusations against him and Job prayed for them, as directed by God:

> "When Job prayed for his friends,
> the Lord restored his fortunes.
> In fact, the Lord gave him twice
> as much as before!
> Then all his brothers, sisters and
> former friends came and feasted
> with him in his home.
> And they consoled him and
> comforted him because of all
> the trials the Lord had brought
> against him. And each of them brought
> him a gift of money and a gold ring.
> So the Lord blessed Job
> in the second half of his life
> even more than the beginning.
> For now he had 14,000 sheep,
> 6,000 camels, 1000 teams of oxen,
> and 1,000 female donkeys.
> He also gave Job seven more sons
> and three more daughters.
> He named his first daughter Jeminah,
> the second Keziah, and the third
> Keren-happuch. In all the land
> no women were as lovely as
> the daughters of Job.
> And their father put them into his will
> along with their brothers.
> Job lived 140 years after that,
> living to see four generations
> of his children and grandchildren.
> Then he died,
> an old man who had lived a long, full life."
> (Job 42:12-17)

Thus in the end, in Job's life, good did indeed triumph over evil.

Looking at his life as a whole Job, to be sure, certainly lived the good life. The moral and religious principles to which he was so deeply and resolutely committed, formed the strong and secure foundation on which his whole life of power, influence and wealth was built. Or so it seemed. Before long, this seemingly durable foundation and the eminently successful life on which it was built collapsed under the crushing weight of multiple tragedies, calamities and suffering. The good life, for all intents and purposes, disappeared suddenly, swiftly and completely. Or did it?

Strangely but truly, this suffering was all part and parcel of Job's good life. And if Job's life had ended at this point—as it almost did—it is questionable whether one could reasonably regard it as the good life. Job, absolutely, did not consider it good. His suffering at one point was so intolerable that he just did not see how he could endure it any longer, and in fact wished that he would die so that the suffering would end:

> "I would rather be strangled—
> rather die than suffer like this.
> I hate my life and don't want
> to go on living.
> Oh, leave me alone,
> for my few remaining days."
> (Job 7:15-16)

His depression and desperation had reached such a troubling stage that he even "cursed the day of his birth"—wished that he had never been born:

> "Let the day of my birth be erased,
> and the night I was conceived.
> Let that day be turned to darkness.
> Let it be lost even to God on high,
> and let no light shine on it.
> Let the darkness and utter gloom
> claim that day for its own.
> Let a black cloud overshadow it,

and let the darkness terrify it.
Let that night
be blotted off the calendar,
never again to be counted
among the days of the year;
never again to appear among the months.
Let that night be childless.
Let it have no joy.
Let those who are experts at cursing—
whose cursing could rouse Leviathan—
curse that day.
Let its morning stars remain dark.
Let it hope for light, but in vain;
may it never see the morning light.
Curse that day
for failing to shut my mother's womb,
for letting me be born
to see all this trouble.
Why wasn't I born dead?
Why didn't I die
as I came from the womb?
Why was I laid on my mother's lap?
Why did she nurse me at her breasts?
Had I died at birth,
I would now be at peace.
I would be asleep and at rest.
I would rest
with the world's kings and prime ministers,
whose great buildings now lie in ruins.
I would rest with princes, rich in gold,
whose palaces were filled with silver.
Why wasn't I buried
like a stillborn child,
like a baby who never lives to see the light?
For in death
the wicked cause no trouble,

and the weary are at rest.
Even captives are at ease in death,
with no guards to curse them.
Rich and poor are both there,
and the slave is free from his master."
(Job 3:3-19)

Job's suffering is a convincing reminder that suffering of one kind or another is an integral part of all human experience. None of us can escape it.

Not even if we are good, as in the case of Job. We may be good but we are not perfect. Our human condition, as a result of our imperfect sinful nature, guarantees that we will experience suffering or trouble in one form or another in the course of our lives. Again, as Eliphaz so aptly expresses it:

"People are born for trouble
as readily as sparks fly from a fire."
(Job 5:7)

To be sure, Job did not take issue with Eliphaz on this point; one of the few areas on which they stood on common ground. Job was not making a claim for perfection, neither was he saying that he qualified for exemption from suffering because of his goodness. Job's argument simply was that, given his own moral imperfection he had done nothing so abhorrently evil in his life to merit this gigantic avalanche of tragedies and calamities that fell so suddenly and mercilessly on him.

Curiously, in God's response to Job after he made his appearance in the whirlwind, even though he knew this was the primary question on Job's mind, God never answers it directly. Neither does Job pursue it with him. And so, rather disappointingly, we get no clear definitive answer from the book of Job as to why so often good people suffer so much in this world.

But perhaps the answer is in Job's ultimate vindication, an action that speaks convincingly much louder than words. And, to be sure, if this is so, then no other answer is necessary. The vindication speaks eloquently and powerfully for itself. The primary point of Job's vindication is not particularly the abundant, tangible blessings that came with it, but the fact that all along God was present and personally involved at every stage of Job's seemingly endless experience of suffering even though, understandably, Job did not realize it, so overcome and overwhelmed he was with his suffering. Job felt totally abandoned by God throughout the entire depressing period of his suffering; at the very time, in other words, when he most desperately needed God. And it is not surprising that Job felt this way, because God gave no clear indication or revelation that he was present with Job during this unbearably bitter and painful period of his life, even though Job earnestly but unsuccessfully pleaded for such a revelation. God's presence meant that he was not just an uncaring bystander, simply observing what was happening in Job's life, but a loving, just and compassionate God who was personally with Job through all his critical and calamitous struggles, and who was just waiting for the right time to intervene for Job's personal good and well-being. In essence, therefore, God's presence guaranteed that Job would triumph in the end and that the whole suffering experience would make Job an even better and stronger person.

This, inevitably perhaps, brings to mind a similar feeling of being abandoned by God that Christ expressed during his suffering on the cross on behalf of sinful humanity. In deepest agony and feeling all alone at this darkest moment of his crucifixion, Jesus, as if in absolute desperation, cried out to God: "My God, my God, why have you abandoned me?"(Matt.27:46)

Humanly speaking, it is difficult to understand why the crucifixion was necessary to bring about the redemption of humanity. Why Jesus had to suffer such a horrible and brutal death on the cross on our behalf will perhaps forever remain a mystery to us. It certainly goes radically against our basic sense of reason and justice. But the fact is that for all the options open to God to accomplish human redemption, in his infinite wisdom and justice, he determined that the crucifixion of Christ was the right, just and best means of realizing it.

To be sure, it is no big surprise that we cannot understand God's justice and reason on this issue, because, as Paul reminds us in the New Testament, the human mind can never fully fathom the deep mysteries of God:

> "Oh, how great are God's riches
> and wisdom and knowledge!
> How impossible it is for us
> to understand his decisions and ways!"
> (Rom. 11:33)

This is precisely why faith is such an absolute necessity if we are to have a good and growing relationship with God:

> "And it is impossible to please God
> without faith. Anyone who wants
> to come to him must believe that
> God exists and that he rewards those
> who sincerely seek him."
> (Heb. 11:6)

Clearly then, one must necessarily conclude that by divine design suffering is an integral part of God's plan for those who are good. In the case of Christ, the only One who was perfectly good, and the only One therefore who could not and did not sin, God assigned him the suffering role to fulfill the divine plan for redemption of all humanity.

Then, in terms of Job, even though, to be sure, he was not perfectly good, yet he was very good, so good in fact that he came as close as anyone could possibly come to moral perfection in that God speaks of him as "the finest man in all the earth." (Job 1:8) To receive such a high commendation from God means that beyond any doubt Job had reached a level of moral integrity, virtue and practical goodness in his personal life that was virtually second to none in the world of his day. Yet, in spite of this, or perhaps because of it, suffering in its most ruinously destructive form was an integral part of Job's good life.

And, of course, we need to remember too that just as Job's life ended not in suffering but in a transforming victory of vindication, the cross was not the end of Christ. Easter was and is the convincing declaration to the world that the resurrection of Christ was the transforming event and triumphant victory for Christ and humanity in God's plan for human redemption.

The wisdom writers also consider, in further explanation of why the good suffer, that in some cases suffering may be one of the methods used by God, as a caring and loving Father, to discipline a good child to make him or her a better person. Since we can never realize moral perfection in this life, no matter how good we are, the potential for moral growth as a person is endless. The author of Proverbs 3 thinks that suffering, sometimes as a form of correction, is a type of discipline that God uses as an instrument to personal moral growth:

> "My child, don't reject the Lord's
> discipline, and don't be upset
> when he corrects you.
> For the Lord corrects those he loves,
> just as a father corrects a child
> in whom he delights."
> (Prov. 3:11-12)

David recognizes that God disciplines him when he sins, and so he pleads that God would not discipline him in divine anger so that, presumably, his punishment or suffering would be mild:

> "O Lord, don't rebuke me
> in your anger or discipline me
> in your rage.
> Have compassion on me, Lord,
> for I am weak.
> Heal me, Lord, for my bones
> are in agony."
> (Psalm 6:1-2)

Eliphaz tells Job that his suffering may be God's way of disciplining him. He should therefore not resent or despise this divine discipline but joyfully welcome it:

"But consider the joy of those
corrected by God!
Do not despise the discipline
of the Almighty when you sin.
For though he wounds,
He also bandages.
He strikes, but his hands also heal."
(Job 5:17-18)

# Chapter 3

## THE CHALLENGE OF THE GOOD LIFE

In summary then, the good life, as the wisdom writers see it, is not a life free from trouble or tragedy, suffering or struggle, crisis or calamity. Indeed, as they reveal, such a life in reality does not exist and is not possible in human terms. Therefore, it is unrealistic and unwise to strive for such a life. Our human condition of imperfection guarantees that we will never be able to realize such an ideal state of trouble-free living, no matter how hard we try. We have all been created in the image of God, to be sure, but it is an image which has been tarnished by our inherently sinful and therefore imperfect nature. This thus ensures that we can never escape evil, in one way or another, in one sense or the other, in the practical course of our every day lives. And so, in pursuit of the good life, we strive to overcome evil in our selves and in the world, wherever and whenever we encounter it.

This ceaseless struggle to triumph over evil within and around us indicates that the moral conflict between good and evil is a battle we are continuously engaged in throughout our lives. Our moral imperfection also reminds us constantly and frustratingly, and even at times fearfully, that there is little in life that we actually do control. Indeed, this is so not just in regard to life in general but in terms of our individual lives in particular.

As we have already noted, our coming into this world was not our decision and, generally speaking, we will have little or no say as to how or when we leave it. Neither do we have a choice as to whether or not to leave it. Death dictates that we all have to leave this world, whether we like it or not.

Because there is so little that we actually do control in terms of the things that really matter in life, even with the best intentions in the world, we are no match for the forces of evil all around us and particularly those within us. We very often find that despite our diligent and determined efforts, we are constantly fighting a losing battle against such evil forces as hate, envy, jealousy, greed, lust, anger, bigotry. Our only hope, the wisdom writers insist, and rightly so, is God.

Indeed, the fact that our human limitations keep us so powerless is in itself a powerful argument for the existence of God. Humanity's powerlessness in so many crucial and critical areas of life, both on a personal level and in general necessarily points to the existence of Someone infinitely superior to humanity who, by virtue of limitless power, controls all that exists. It points to and implies, in other words, the existence of Someone who is the infinite Creator, and thus ultimate Controller, of everything and everyone—the existence, that is, of God:

> "When I look at the night sky
> and see the work of your fingers—
> the moon and the stars you set in place—
> what are mere mortals
> that you should think about them,
> human beings that you should care for them?
> Yet you made them
> only a little lower than God
> and crowned them with glory and honor.
> You gave them charge
> of everything you made,
> putting all things under their authority—
> the flocks and the herds
> and all the wild animals,
> the birds in the sky,
> the fish in the sea, and
> everything that swims the ocean currents.
> O Lord, our Lord,
> your majestic name fills the earth!"
> (Psalm 8:3-9)

Thus, if we are serious about living the good life, our good intentions, while a necessary first step, would not by themselves suffice. A key factor that would enable us to realize the goal of the good life is that we should consistently strive to overcome evil in all of its many forms and disguises. But we cannot achieve this objective just by our own will power. The wisdom writers remind us time and again that we underestimate the power of evil, in particular the evil in our own lives, at our own peril. We need the moral power from within, which God generously bestows on all who genuinely seek it, to successfully and triumphantly cope with evil in all its various manifestations.

David, as we have already noted, was a great military and spiritual leader; unquestionably, the greatest military genius in Israel's history. But though he had accomplished an impressive and incredible record of conquests on the military battlefield, on the moral battlefield of the heart David discovered that, on his own, he was no match for the powerful and seductive forces of evil, as his adultery with Bathsheba clearly revealed. Lust conquered David's heart and lust led to adultery. Deeply overcome with guilt and remorse for the gravity of his sin, David realized that to win this moral battle within he definitely needed divine help. And so in his very sincere and earnest prayer for forgiveness in Psalm 51, David also appealed to God for the moral purity and power within that would enable him to prevail in conflicts of the heart:

> "Create in me a clean heart, O God.
> Renew a loyal spirit within me."
> (Psalm 51:10)

Then, of course, the most effective weapon we have in the fight to overcome evil is to do good. But doing good, for the most part, is easier said than done. So much so, in fact, that even the best among us, from time to time, need practical help and guidance as we strive for the good in our lives, in the community and in the world.

In the following chapters, therefore, we have the timeless wisdom and insights of the wisdom writers on a variety of themes and topics in the hope that they would challenge and inspire us to do the good and the right and, in the process, help us to realize the most worthy goal of the good life.

(In quotations from the book of Job, when the name of the speaker is omitted it means that the speaker is Job )

# Chapter 4

## ABANDON

My God, my God
why have you abandoned me?
Why are you so far away when I groan for help?
Every day I call to you, my God,
but you do not answer.
Every night you hear my voice,
but I find no relief.
(Psalm 22:1-2)

Even if my father and mother abandon me,
the Lord will hold me close.
(Psalm 27:10)

O Lord, you know all about this.
Do not stay silent.
Do not abandon me now, Lord.
Wake up! Rise to my defense!
Take up my case, my God and my Lord.
(Psalm 35:22-23)

Do not abandon me, O Lord.
Do not stand at a distance, my God.
Come quickly to help me,
O Lord, my Savior.
(Psalm 38:21-22)

Help me abandon my shameful ways;
for your regulations are good.
(Psalm 119:39)

## ACCEPT

Accept the way God does things,
for who can straighten
what he has made crooked?
(Eccles. 7:13)

## ADULTERY(ADULTERER)

The adulterer waits for the twilight, saying,
'No one will see me then.'
He hides his face so no one will know him.
(Job 24:15)

For a prostitute will bring you to poverty,
but sleeping with another man's wife
will cost you your life.
Can a man scoop a flame into his lap
and not have his clothes catch on fire?
Can he walk on hot coals
and not blister his feet?
So it is with the man
who sleeps with another man's wife.
He who embraces her
will not go unpunished.
Excuses might be found for a thief
who steals because he is starving.
But if he is caught, he must pay back
seven times what he stole,
even if he has to sell everything in his house.
But the man who commits adultery
is an utter fool,
for he destroys himself.
He will be wounded and disgraced.
His shame will never be erased.
For the woman's jealous husband
will be furious, and he will show no mercy
when he takes revenge.
He will accept no compensation,
nor be satisfied with a payoff of any size.
(Prov. 6:26-35)

## ADVICE

They rejected my advice
and paid no attention
when I corrected them.
Therefore they must eat the bitter fruit
of living their own way,
choking on their own schemes.
( Prov. 1:30-31)

People who despise advice
are asking for trouble;
those who respect a command will succeed.
(Prov. 13:13)

Plans go wrong for lack of advice;
many advisers bring success.
(Prov. 15:22)

Get all the advice and instruction you can,
so you will be wise the rest of your life.
(Prov. 19:20)

Though good advice lies deep within the heart,
a person with understanding will draw it out.
(Prov. 20:5)

Plans succeed through good counsel;
don't go to war without wise advice.
(Prov. 20:18)

Don't waste your breath on fools,
for they will despise the wisest advice.
(Prov. 23:9)

Timely advice is lovely,
like golden apples in a silver basket.
(Prov. 25:11)

## ALCOHOL

Wine produces mockers;
alcohol leads to brawls.
Those led astray by drink cannot be wise.
(Prov. 20:1)

## ALONE

Two people are better off than one,
for they can help each other succeed.
If one person falls,
the other can reach out and help.
But someone who falls alone
is in real trouble.
Likewise, two people lying close together
can keep each other warm.
But how can one be warm alone?
A person standing alone
can be attacked and defeated,
but two can stand back-to-back and conquer.
Three are even better,
for a triple-braided cord is not easily broken.
(Eccles. 4:9-12)

## ANGEL

For the angel of the Lord is a guard;
he surrounds and defends
all who fear him.
(Psalm 34:7)

## ANGER(ANGRY)

Don't sin by letting anger control you.
Think about it overnight and remain silent.
(Psalm 4:4)

O Lord, don't rebuke me in your anger
or discipline me in your rage.
Have compassion on me Lord, for I am weak.
( Psalm 6:1-2)

Arise O Lord in anger!
Stand up against the fury of my enemies!
Wake up, my God, and bring justice!
(Psalm 7:6)

Do not turn your back on me.
Do not reject your servant in anger.
You have always been my helper.
Don't leave me now;
don't abandon me,
O God of my salvation.
(Psalm 27:9)

Sing to the Lord, all you godly ones!
Praise his holy name.
For his anger lasts only a moment,
but his favor lasts a lifetime!
Weeping may last through the night,
but joy comes with the morning.
(Psalm 30:4-5)

Stop being angry!
Turn from your rage!
Do not lose your temper—
it only leads to harm
(Psalm 37:8)

But you, O Lord,
are a God of compassion and mercy,
slow to get angry
and filled with unfailing love and faithfulness.
(Psalm 86:15)

The Lord is compassionate and merciful,
slow to get angry
and filled with unfailing love.
He will not constantly accuse us,
nor remain angry forever.
(Psalm 103:8-9)

People with understanding
control their anger;
a hot temper shows great foolishness.
(Prov. 14:29)

A gentle answer deflects anger
but harsh words make tempers flare.
(Prov. 15:1)

People ruin their lives
by their own foolishness,
and then are angry at the Lord.
(Prov. 19:3)

Don't befriend angry people
or associate with hot-tempered people,
or you will learn to be like them
and endanger your soul.
(Prov. 22:24-25)

An angry person starts fights;
a hot-tempered person
commits all kinds of sin.
(Prov. 29:22)

Control your temper,
for anger labels you a fool.
(Eccles. 7:9)

## ANIMAL(S)

The godly care for their animals,
but the wicked are always cruel.
(Prov. 12:10)

## AVOID EXTREMES

I have seen everything in this meaningless life,
including the death of good young people,
and the long life of wicked people.
So don't be too good or too wise!
Why destroy yourself?
On the other hand, don't be too wicked.
Don't be a fool!
Why die before your time.
Pay attention to these instructions,
for anyone who fears God will avoid both extremes.
(Eccles. 7:15-18)

# Chapter 5

# B

## BAD

But Job replied,
"You talk like a foolish woman.
Should we accept only good things
from the hand of God
and never anything bad?"
So in all this Job said nothing wrong.
(Job 2:10)

## BEAUTY

Charm is deceptive, and beauty does not last;
but a woman who fears the Lord
will be greatly praised.
Reward her for all she has done.
Let her deeds publicly declare her praise.
(Prov. 31:30-31)

## BIRTH

"Why then did you deliver me
from my mother's womb?
Why didn't you let me die at birth?
It would be as though I had never existed,
going directly from the womb to the grave."
(Job 10:18-19)

## BLESSED

When Job prayed for his friends,
the Lord restored his fortunes.
In fact the Lord gave him
twice as much as before!
So the Lord blessed Job in the second half
of his life even more than in the beginning.
(Job 42:10,12)

## BLESSING(S)

You prepare a feast for me
in the presence of my enemies
You honor me by anointing my head with oil.
My cup overflows with blessings.
(Psalm 23:5)

With all my heart I want your blessings
Be merciful as you promised.
(Psalm 119:58)

The blessing of the Lord makes a person rich,
and he adds no sorrow with it.
(Prov. 10:22)

Trouble chases sinners,
while blessings reward the righteous.
(Prov. 13:21)

## BRIBE(S)

Don't let me suffer the fate of sinners.
Don't condemn me along with murderers.
Their hands are dirty with evil schemes,
and they constantly take bribes.
(Psalm 26:9-10)

Extortion turns wise people into fools,
and bribes corrupt the heart.
(Eccles. 7:7)

## BROKENHEARTED

The Lord is close to the brokenhearted;
he rescues those whose spirits are crushed.
(Psalm 34:18)

# Chapter 6

# C

## CHANCE

I have observed something else under the sun.
The fastest runner doesn't always win the race,
and the strongest warrior
doesn't always win the battle.
The wise sometimes go hungry,
and the skillful are not necessarily wealthy.
And those who are educated
don't always lead successful lives.
It is all decided by chance,
by being in the right place at the right time.
(Eccles. 9:11)

## CHILD(REN)

Children are a gift from the Lord;
they are a reward from him.
(Psalm 127:3)

A wise child brings joy to a father;
a foolish child brings grief to a mother.
(Prov. 10:1)

Discipline your children while there is hope.
Otherwise you will ruin their lives.
(Prov. 19:18)

Children who mistreat their father
or chase away their mother
are an embarrassment and a public disgrace.
(Prov. 19:26)

Even children are known
by the way they act,
whether their conduct is pure,
and whether it is right.
(Prov. 20:11)

The father of godly children has cause for joy.
What a pleasure
to have children who are wise.
So give your father and mother joy!
May she who gave you birth be happy.
(Prov. 23:24-25)

## CITY

Upright citizens are good for a city
and make it prosper,
but the talk of the wicked tears it apart.
(Prov. 11:11)

## COMFORT

"At least I can take comfort in this:
Despite the pain,
I have not denied the words of the Holy One."
(Job 6:10)

## COMMAND(COMMANDMENTS)

"For I have stayed on God's paths;
I have followed his ways and not turned aside.
I have not departed from his commands,
but have treasured his words
more than daily food."
(Job 23:11-12)

You have charged us
to keep your commandments carefully.
Oh, that my actions
would consistently reflect your decrees.
(Psalm 119:4-5)

You rebuke the arrogant;
those who wander from your commands are cursed.
(Psalm 119:21)

Help me understand
the meaning of your commandments,
and I will meditate on your wonderful deeds.
(Psalm 119:27)

I long to obey your commandments!
Renew my life with your goodness.
(Psalm 119:40)

How I delight in your commands!
How I love them!
I honor and love your commands.
I meditate on your decrees.
(Psalm 119:47-48)

You made me, you created me.
Now give me the sense to follow your commands.
(Psalm 119:73)

All your commands are trustworthy.
(Psalm 119:86)

Give me a helping hand,
for I have chosen to follow your commandments.
(Psalm 119:173)

Keep the commandments and keep your life;
despising them leads to death.
(Prov. 19:16)

## COMMIT

Commit everything you do to the Lord.
Trust him, and he will help you.
He will make your innocence
radiate like the dawn
and the justice of your cause
will shine like the noonday sun.
(Psalm 37:5-6)

## COMMON SENSE

My child, don't lose sight of common sense
and discernment.
Hang on to them, for they will refresh your soul.
They are like jewels on a necklace.
They keep you safe on your way,
and your feet will not stumble.
You can go to bed without fear;
you will lie down and sleep soundly.
(Prov. 3:21-24)

The person who strays from common sense
will end up in the company of the dead.
(Prov. 21:16)

## COMPASSION(COMPASSIONATE)

O Lord, don't rebuke me in your anger
or discipline me in your rage.
Have compassion on me, Lord, for I am weak.
(Psalm 6:1-2)

Remember, O Lord,
your compassion and unfailing love,
which you have shown from long ages past.
(Psalm 25:6)

The Lord is like a father to his children,
tender and compassionate to those who fear him.
(Psalm 103:13)

Light shines in the darkness for the godly.
They are generous, compassionate and righteous.
(Psalm 112:4)

The Lord is merciful and compassionate,
slow to get angry and filled with unfailing love.
(Psalm 146:8)

## COMPLAINT

"My complaint is with God, not with people.
I have good reason to be so impatient."
(Job 21:4)

"My complaint today is still a bitter one,
and I try hard not to groan aloud.
If only I knew where to find God,
I would go to his court.
I would lay out my case and present my arguments."
(Job 23:2-4)

## CONFLICT

Better a dry crust eaten in peace
than a house filled with feasting—and conflict.
(Prov. 17:1)

## CORNERSTONE

The stone that the builders rejected
has now become the cornerstone.
This is the Lord's doing, and it is wonderful to see.
(Psalm 118:22-23)

## CORRUPT

Corrupt people walk a thorny and treacherous road;
whoever values life will avoid it.
(Prov. 22:5)

## COURAGE

"Having hope will give you courage."(Zophar)
(Job 11:18)

## CRITICISM

If you ignore criticism,
you will end in poverty and disgrace;
if you accept correction, you will be honored.
(Prov. 13:18)

If you listen to constructive criticism,
you will be at home among the wise.
(Prov. 15:13)

In the end,
people appreciate honest criticism
far more than flattery.
(Prov. 28:23)

## CURSE

His wife said to him,
"Are you still trying to maintain your integrity?
Curse God and die."
(Job 2:9)

# Chapter 7

# D

## DEATH(DEAD)

"For in death the wicked cause no trouble,
and the weary are at rest.
Even captives are at ease in death,
with no guards to curse them.
Rich and poor are both there,
and the slave is free from his master."
(Job 3:17-19)

"If he snatches someone in death,
who can stop him?
Who dares to ask, 'What are you doing?'"
(Job 9:12)

"Can the dead live again?
If so, this would give me hope
through all my years of struggle
and I would eagerly await the release of death."
(Job 14:14)

Return, O Lord, and rescue me.
Save me because of your unfailing love.
For the dead do not remember you.
Who can praise you from the grave?
(Psalm 6:4-5)

I also thought about the human condition—
how God proves to people
that they are like animals.
For people and animals share the same fate—
both breathe and both die.
So people have no real advantage
over the animals.
How meaningless!
Both go to the same place—
they came from dust—
they return to dust.
For who can prove
that the human spirit goes up
and the spirit of animals
goes down into the earth?
So I saw that there is nothing better for people
than to be happy in their work.
That is why we are here!
No one will bring us back from death
to enjoy life after we die.
(Eccles.3:18-22)

A wise person thinks a lot about death,
while a fool thinks
only about having a good time.
(Eccles. 7:4)

## DEEDS

The seeds of good deeds become a tree of life;
a wise person wins friends.
(Prov. 11:30)

## DESTINY

Everything has already been decided.
It was known long ago
what each person would be.
So there's no use arguing with God
about your destiny.
(Eccles. 6:10)

## DICE

We may throw the dice;
but the Lord determines how they fall.
(Prov. 16:33)

## DISCERNMENT

My child,
don't lose sight of common sense and discernment.
Hang on to them,
for they will refresh your soul.
They are like jewels on a necklace.
They keep you safe on your way,
and your feet will not stumble.
You can go to bed without fear;
you will lie down and sleep soundly.
(Prov. 3:21-24)

## DISCIPLINE

"But consider the joy of those corrected by God!
Do not despise the discipline of the Almighty
when you sin.
For though he wounds,
he also bandages.
He strikes but his hands also heals."(Eliphaz)
(Job 5:17-18)

"Or God disciplines people with pain
on their sickbeds,
with ceaseless aching in their bones."(Elihu)
(Job 33:19)

O Lord, don't rebuke me in your anger
or discipline me in your rage.
Have compassion on me, Lord,
for I am weak.
Heal me, Lord, for my bones are in agony.
(Psalm 6:1-2)

Joyful are those you discipline, Lord,
those you teach with your instructions.
(Psalm 94:12)

My child, don't reject the Lord's discipline,
and don't be upset when he corrects you.
For the Lord corrects those he loves,
just as a father
corrects a child in whom he delights.
(Prov. 3:11-12)

My son, obey your father's commands,
and don't neglect your mother's instruction.
Keep their words always in your heart.
Tie them around your neck.
When you walk,
their counsel will lead you.
When you sleep, they will protect you.
When you wake up, they will advise you.
For their command is a lamp
and their instruction a light;
their corrective discipline is the way to life.
(Prov. 6:20-23)

People who accept discipline
are on the pathway to life,
but those who ignore correction
will go astray.
(Prov. 10:17)

To learn, you must love discipline;
it is stupid to hate correction.
(Prov. 12:1)

A wise child accepts a parent's discipline,
a mocker refuses to listen to correction.
(Prov. 13:1)

Those who spare the rod of discipline
hate their children.
Those who love their children
care enough to discipline them.
(Prov. 13:24)

If you reject discipline,
you only harm yourself;
but if you listen to correction
you grow in understanding.
(Prov. 15:32)

Physical punishment cleanses away evil;
such discipline purifies the heart.
(Prov. 20:30)

A youngster's heart is filled with foolishness,
but physical discipline will drive it far away.
(Prov. 22:15)

Don't fail to discipline your children.
They won't die if you spank them.
Physical discipline may well
save them from death.
(Prov. 23:13-14)

Discipline your children,
and they will give you peace of mind
and will make your heart glad.
(Prov. 29:17)

## DISCRETION

A beautiful woman who lacks discretion
is like a gold ring in a pig's snout.
(Prov. 11:22)

Discretion is a life-giving fountain
to those who possess it,
but discipline is wasted on fools.
(Prov. 16:22)

## DO WELL

Whatever you do, do well.
For when you go to the grave
there will be no work,
or planning or knowledge or wisdom.
(Eccles. 9:10)

## DOUBLE STANDARD

False weights and unequal measures—
the Lord detests double standards of every kind.
(Prov. 20:10)

# Chapter 8

## EARTH(WORLD)

O Lord, our Lord,
your majestic name fills the earth!
Your glory is higher than the heavens.
(Psalm 8:1)

He watches everyone closely,
examining every person on earth.
The Lord examines
both the righteous and the wicked.
He hates those who love violence.
(Psalm 11:4-5)

Help, O Lord,
for the godly are fast disappearing!
The faithful have vanished from the earth!
Neighbors lie to each other,
speaking with flattering lips and deceitful hearts.
(Psalm 12:1-2)

The heavens proclaim the glory of God.
The skies display his craftsmanship.
Day after day they continue to speak;
night after night they make him known.
They speak without a sound or word;
Their voice is never heard.
Yet their message has gone throughout the earth,
and their words to all the world.
(Psalm 19:1-4)

The earth is the Lord's and everything in it.
The world and all its people belong to him.
(Psalm 24:1)

Let the whole world fear the Lord,
and let everyone stand in awe of him.
(Psalm 33:8)

Be still and know that I am God!
I will be honored by every nation.
I will be honored throughout the world.
(Psalm 46:10)

Be exalted, O God, above the highest heavens!
May your glory shine over all the earth.
(Psalm 57:5)

You are the hope of everyone on earth,
even those who sail on distant seas.
(Psalm 65:5)

Shout joyful praises to God, all the earth!
Sing about the glory of his name!
Tell the world how glorious he is.
(Psalm 66:1-2)

Let the whole world bless our God
and loudly sing his praises.
Our lives are in his hands,
and he keeps our feet from stumbling.
(Psalm 66:8-9)

May your ways be known
throughout the earth,
your saving power among people everywhere.
(Psalm 67:2)

Let the whole earth be filled with his glory.
(Psalm 72:19)

He is coming to judge the earth.
He will judge the world with justice,
and the nations with his truth.
(Psalm 96:13)

For you, O Lord, are supreme over all the earth;
you are exalted far above all gods.
(Psalm 97:9)

Praise the Lord, all you nations.
Praise him, all you people of the earth.
For he loves us with unfailing love;
the Lord's faithfulness endures forever.
(Psalm 117:1-2)

## EAVESDROP

Don't eavesdrop on others—
you may hear your servant curse you.
For you know how often
you yourself have cursed others.
(Eccles. 7:21-22)

## ENDURE

"But I don't have the strength to endure.
I have nothing to live for."
(Job 6:11)

## ENEMY(ENEMIES)

The Lord has heard my plea;
The Lord will answer my prayer.
May all my enemies be disgraced and terrified.
May they suddenly turn back in shame.
(Psalm 6:9-10)

Arise, O Lord, in anger!
Stand up against the fury of my enemies.
Wake up, my God, and bring justice.
(Psalm 7:6)

O Lord, how long will you forget me?
Forever?
How long will you look the other way?
How long must I struggle
with anguish in my soul,
with sorrow in my heart every day?
How long will my enemy have the upper hand?
(Psalm 13:1-2)

By your mighty power you rescue those
who seek refuge from their enemies.
(Psalm 17:7)

You prepare a feast for me
in the presence of my enemies.
You honor me
by anointing my head with oil.
My cup overflows with blessings.
(Psalm 23:5)

Don't rejoice when your enemies fall.
Don't be happy when they stumble.
For the Lord will be displeased with you
and will turn his anger away from them
(Prov. 24: 17-18)

If your enemies are hungry,
give them food to eat.
If they are thirsty,
give them water to drink.
You will heap burning coals of shame
on their heads,
and the Lord will reward you.
(Prov. 25: 21-22)

## ENJOY

Even so, I have noticed one thing, at least,
that is good.
It is good for people to eat, drink
and enjoy their work under the sun
during the short life God has given them,
and to accept their lot in life.
And it is a good thing
to receive wealth from God
and the good health to enjoy it.
To enjoy your work
and to accept your lot in life—
this is indeed a gift from God.
God keeps such people so busy enjoying life
that they take no time to brood over the past.
(Eccles. 5:18-20)

Enjoy what you have
rather than desiring what you don't have.
Just dreaming about nice things
is meaningless—like chasing the wind.
(Eccles. 6:9)

## ENVY

Don't worry about the wicked
or envy those who do wrong.
For like grass, they soon fade away.
Like spring flowers, they soon wither.
(Psalm 37:1-2)

But as for me, I almost lost my footing.
My feet were slipping,
and I was almost gone.
For I envied the proud
when I saw them prosper
despite their wickedness.
They seem to live such painless lives,
their bodies are so healthy and strong.
They don't have troubles like other people;
they're not plagued with problems
like everyone else.
(Psalm 73:2-5)

Don't envy violent people or copy their ways.
Such wicked people are detestable to the Lord,
but he offers his friendship to the godly.
(Prov. 3:31-32)

Don't envy sinners,
but always continue to fear the Lord.
You will be rewarded for this;
your hope will not be disappointed.
(Prov. 23:17-18)

Don't envy evil people
or desire their company.
For their hearts plot violence,
and their words always stir up trouble.
(Prov. 24:1-2)

Don't fret because of evildoers;
don't envy the wicked.
For evil people have no future;
the light of the wicked will be snuffed out.
(Prov. 24:19-20)

## EVIL

"My experience shows
that those who plant trouble and cultivate evil
will harvest the same."(Eliphaz)
(Job 4:8)

"But ask those who have been around,
and they will tell you the truth.
Evil people are spared in times of calamity
and are allowed to escape disaster."
(Job 21:29-30)

O God, you take no pleasure in wickedness;
you cannot tolerate the sins of the wicked.
Therefore, the proud may not stand
in your presence,
for you hate all who do evil.
(Psalm 5:4-5)

End the evil of those who are wicked,
and defend the righteous.
For you look deep within the mind and heart,
O righteous God.
(Psalm 7:9)

The wicked conceive evil;
they are pregnant with trouble
and give birth to lies.
They dig a deep pit to trap others,
then fall into it themselves.
The trouble they make for others
backfires on them.
The violence they plan falls on their own heads.
(Psalm 7:14-16)

The wicked arrogantly hunt down the poor.
Let them be caught
in the evil they plan for others.
For they brag about their evil desires;
they praise the greedy and curse the Lord.
(Psalm 10:2-3)

Does anyone want to live a life
that is long and prosperous?
Then keep your tongue from speaking evil
and your lips from telling lies.
(Psalm 34:12-13)

Good comes to those
who lend money generously
and conduct their business fairly.
Such people will not be overcome by evil.
(Psalm 112:5-6)

For evil people cannot sleep
until they've done their evil deed for the day.
They cannot rest until they've caused
someone to stumble.
They eat the food of wickedness
and drink the wine of violence.
(Prov. 4:16-17)

An evil man is held captive by his own sins;
they are ropes that catch and hold him.
He will die for lack of self-control;
he will be lost
because of his great foolishness.
(Prov. 5:22-23)

The earnings of the godly enhance their lives,
but evil people squander their money on sin.
(Prov. 10:16)

Evil people get rich for the moment,
but the reward of the godly will last.
(Prov. 11:21)

The Lord is watching everywhere,
keeping his eye on both the evil and the good.
(Prov. 15:3)

If you repay good with evil,
evil will never leave your house.
(Prov. 17:3)

There is another evil I have seen under the sun.
Kings and rulers make a grave mistake
when they give great authority
to foolish people and low positions
to people of proven worth.
(Eccles. 10:5-6)

# Chapter 9

## FAIL

If you fail under pressure,
your strength is too small.
(Prov. 24:10)

## FAIR(FAIRNESS)

For you have judged in my favor;
From your throne you have judged with fairness.
(Psalm 9:4)

But the Lord reigns forever,
executing judgment from his throne.
He will judge the world with justice
and rule the nations with fairness.
(Psalm 9:7-8)

Reverence for the Lord is pure,
lasting forever.
The laws of the Lord are true;
each one is fair.
They are more desirable than gold,
even the finest gold.
They are sweeter than honey,
even honey dripping from the comb.
They are a warning to your servant,
a great reward for those who obey them.
(Psalm 19:9-11)

Tell all the nations, "The Lord reigns!"
The world stands firm and cannot be shaken.
He will judge all peoples fairly.
(Psalm 96:10)

Mighty King, lover of justice
you have established fairness.
(Psalm 99:4)

I know, O Lord, that your regulations are fair;
you disciplined me because I needed it.
(Psalm 119:75)

O Lord, you are righteous,
and your regulations are fair.
(Psalm 119:137)

## FAITHFUL(FAITHFULNESS)

To the faithful you show yourself faithful;
to those with integrity you show integrity.
(Psalm 18:25)

The Lord leads with unfailing love and faithfulness
all who keep his covenant and obey his demands.
(Psalm 25:10)

I entrust my spirit into your hand.
Rescue me, Lord, for you are a faithful God.
(Psalm 31:5)

Your unfailing love, O Lord,
is as vast as the heavens.
Your faithfulness reaches beyond the clouds.
(Psalm 36:5)

Lord, don't hold back
your tender mercies from me.
Let your unfailing love and faithfulness
always protect.
(Psalm 40:11)

Then I will praise you with music on the harp
because you are faithful to your promises,
O my God.
(Psalm 71:22)

But you, O Lord,
are a God of compassion and mercy,
slow to get angry,
and filled with unfailing love and faithfulness.
(Psalm 86:15)

I will sing of the Lord's unfailing love forever!
Young and old will hear of your faithfulness.
Your unfailing love will last forever.
Your faithfulness is as enduring as the heavens.
(Psalm 89:1-2)

O Lord God of Heaven's Armies!
Where is there anyone
as mighty as you, O Lord?
You are entirely faithful.
(Psalm 89:8)

I have chosen to be faithful;
I have determined to live by your regulations.
(Psalm 119:30)

Your faithfulness extends to every generation,
as enduring as the earth you created.
(Psalm 119:90)

In your faithful love, O Lord, hear my cry:
Let me be revived
by following your regulations.
(Psalm 119:149)

All of your works will thank you, Lord,
and your faithful followers will praise you.
(Psalm 145:10)

He guards the path of the just
and protects those who are faithful to him.
(Prov. 2:8)

## FAMILY(FAMILIES)

"My family is gone
and my close friends have forgotten me."
(Job 19:14)

"My breath is repulsive to my wife.
I am rejected by my own family."
(Job 19:17)

Those who bring trouble on their families
inherit the wind.
The fool will be a servant to the wise.
(Prov. 11:29)

## FAVORITISM

It is wrong to show favoritism when passing judgment.
(Prov. 24:23)

## FEAR(AFRAID)

"We cannot imagine the power of the Almighty;but even though he is just and righteous,
he does not destroy us.
No wonder people everywhere fear him.
All who are wise show him reverence."(Elihu)
(Job 37:23-24)

The Lord is a friend to those who fear him.
He teaches them his covenant.
(Psalm 25:14)

The Lord is my light and my salvation—
so why should I be afraid?
The Lord is my fortress,
protecting me from danger,
so why should I tremble?
(Psalm 27:1)

Though a mighty army surrounds me,
my heart will not be afraid.
Even if I am attacked,
I will remain confident.
(Psalm 27:3)

I prayed to the Lord and he answered me.
He freed me from all my fears.
(Psalm 34:4)

Fear the Lord, you his godly people,
for those who fear him will have all they need.
(Psalm 34:9)

God is our refuge and strength,
always ready to help in times of trouble.
So we will not fear when earthquakes come
and the mountains crumble into the sea.
(Psalm 46:1-2)

I praise God for what he has promised.
I trust in God, so why should I be afraid?
What can mere mortals do to me?
(Psalm 56:4)

Surely his salvation is near
to those who fear him,
so our land will be filled with his glory.
(Psalm 85:9)

Fear of the Lord
is the foundation of true wisdom.
All who obey his commandments
will grow in wisdom.
(Psalm 110:10)

The Lord is for me, so I will have no fear.
What can mere people do to me?
(Psalm 118:6)

He grants the desires of those who fear him;
he hears their cries for help and rescues them.
(Psalm 145:19)

Fear of the Lord
is the foundation of true knowledge,
but fools despise wisdom and discipline.
(Prov. 1:7)

Fear of the Lord
is the foundation of wisdom.
Knowledge of the Holy One
results in good judgment.
(Prov. 9:10)

Those who fear the Lord are secure;
he will be a refuge for their children.
(Prov. 14:26)

Fear of the Lord is a life-giving fountain;
it offers escape from the snares of death.
(Prov. 14:27)

Better to have little, with the fear of the Lord,
than to have great treasure and turmoil.
(Prov. 15:16)

Fear of the Lord leads to life,
bringing security and protection from harm.
(Prov. 19:23)

## FIGHT(S)

Avoiding a fight is a mark of honor;
only fools insist on quarrelling.
(Prov. 20:3)

A quarrelsome person starts fights
as easily as hot embers light charcoal
or fire lights wood.
(Prov. 26:21)

## FINAL CONCLUSION

That's the whole story.
Here now is my final conclusion:
Fear God and obey his commands,
for this is everyone's duty.
God will judge us for everything we do,
including every secret thing,
whether good or bad.
(Eccles. 12:13-14)

## FINISHING

Finishing is better than starting.
(Eccles. 7:8)

## FOOL(FOOLISHNESS)

"Surely resentment destroys the fool,
and jealousy kills the simple.
I have seen that fools
may be successful for the moment,
but then comes sudden disaster."(Eliphaz)
(Job 5:2-3)

Only fools say in their hearts, "There is no God."
They are corrupt, and there actions are evil;
not one of them does good!
(Psalm 14:1;53:1)

Fear of the Lord
is the foundation of true knowledge,
but fools despise wisdom and discipline.
(Prov. 1:7)

Fools are destroyed by their own complacency.
(Prov. 1:32)

The wise inherit honor,
but fools are put to shame!
(Prov. 3:35)

Doing wrong is fun for a fool,
but living wisely
brings pleasure to the sensible.
(Prov. 10:23)

Fools think their own way is right,
but the wise listen to others.
(Prov. 12:15)

A fool is quick-tempered,
but a wise person stays calm when insulted.
(Prov. 12:16)

The wise are cautious and avoid danger;
fools plunge ahead with reckless confidence.
(Prov. 14:16)

It is safer to meet a bear robbed of her cubs
than to confront a fool caught in foolishness.
(Prov. 17:12)

Even fools are thought wise
when they keep silent;
with their mouths shut,
they seem intelligent.
(Prov. 17:28)

The mouths of fools are their ruin;
they trap themselves with their lips.
(Prov. 18:7)

Honor is no more associated with fools
than snow with summer or rain with harvest.
(Prov. 26:1)

Don't answer the foolish arguments of fools,
or you will become as foolish as they are.
(Prov. 26:4)

Be sure to answer the foolish arguments of fools,
or they will become wise in their own estimation.
(Prov. 26:5)

As dead flies
cause even a bottle of perfume to stink,
so a little foolishness
spoils great wisdom and honor.
(Eccles. 10:1)

Wise words bring approval,
but fools are destroyed by their own words.
(Eccles. 10:12)

## FORGIVE(FORGIVENESS)

Though we are overwhelmed by our sins,
you forgive them all.
(Psalm 65:3)

Help us, O God of our salvation!
Help us for the glory of your name.
Save us and forgive our sins
for the honor of your name.
(Psalm 79:9)

O Lord, you are so good, so ready to forgive,
so full of unfailing love
for all who ask for your help.
(Psalm 86:5)

He forgives all my sins
and heals all my diseases.
(Psalm 103:3)

Lord, if you kept a record of our sins,
who, O Lord, could ever survive?
But you offer forgiveness,
that we might learn to fear you.
(Psalm 130:3-4)

## FOUNDATION(S)

The foundations of law and order have collapsed.
What can the righteous do?
(Psalm 11:3)

When the storms of life come,
the wicked are whirled away,
but the godly have a lasting foundation.
(Prov. 10:25)

## FREEDOM

I will walk in freedom,
for I have devoted myself to your commandments.
(Psalm 119:45)

## FRIEND(S)

"My relatives stay far away,
and my friends have turned against me.
My family is gone,
and my close friends have forgotten me."
(Job 19:13-14)

"My close friends detest me.
Those I have loved have turned against me."
(Job 19:19)

Those who refuse to gossip
or harm their neighbors
or speak evil of their friends.
Those who despise flagrant sinners,
and honor the faithful followers of the Lord,
and keep their promises
even when it hurts.
Those who lend money
without charging interest,
and who cannot be bribed
to lie about the innocent.
Such people will stand firm forever.
(Psalm 15:3-5)

The Lord is a friend to those who fear him.
He teaches them his covenant.
(Psalm 25:14)

Even my best friend,
the one I trusted completely,
the one who shared my food,
has turned against me.
(Psalm 41:9)

I am a friend to anyone who fears you—
anyone who obeys your commandments.
(Psalm 119:63)

The godly give good advice to their friends;
the wicked lead them astray.
(Prov. 12:26)

An offended friend is harder to win back
than a fortified city.
Arguments separate friends
like a gate locked with bars.
(Prov. 18:19)

There are "friends" who destroy each other,
but a real friend sticks closer than a brother.
(Prov. 18:24)

The relatives of the poor despise them;
how much more will their friends avoid them!
Though the poor plead with them,
their friends are gone.
(Prov. 19:7)

Many will say they are loyal friends,
but who can find one who is truly reliable?
(Prov. 20:6)

Just as damaging as a madman
shooting a deadly weapon,
is someone who lies to a friend
and then says, "I was only joking."
(Prov. 26:18-19)

Wounds from a sincere friend
are better than many kisses from an enemy.
(Prov. 27:6)

The heartfelt counsel of a friend
is as sweet as perfume and incense.
(Prov. 27:9)

As iron sharpens iron,
so a friend sharpens a friend.
(Prov. 27:17)

## FUN

So I recommend having fun,
because there is nothing better
for people in this world
than to eat, drink and enjoy life.
That way they will experience some happiness
along with all the hard work
God gives them under the sun.
(Eccles. 8:15)

## FUTURE

No one really knows what is going to happen;
no one can predict the future.
(Eccles. 10:14)

# Chapter 10

# G

## GATEKEEPER

A single day in your courts is better than
a thousand anywhere else!
I would rather be a gatekeeper in the house
of my God than live the good life
in the homes of the wicked.
(Psalm 84:10)

## GENEROUS

The generous will prosper;
Those who refresh others will themselves be refreshed.
(Prov. 11:25)

Blessed are those who are generous,
because they feed the poor.
(Prov. 22:9)

## GET EVEN

Don't say, "I will get even for this wrong."
Wait for the Lord to handle the matter.
(Prov. 20:22)

## GIVE

Give freely and become more wealthy;
be stingy and lose everything.
(Prov. 11:24)

Some people are always greedy for more,
but the godly love to give!
(Prov. 21:26)

## GIFT(S)

Giving a gift can open doors;
it gives access to important people!
(Prov. 18:16)

Many seek favors from a ruler;
everyone is the friend of a person who gives gifts.
(Prov. 19:6)

A secret gift calms anger;
a bribe under the table pacifies fury.
(Prov. 21:14)

A person who promises a gift
but doesn't give it,
is like clouds and wind that bring no rain.
(Prov. 25:14)

What do people really get for all their hard work?
I have seen the burden God has placed on us all.
Yet God has made everything beautiful
for its own time.
He has planted eternity in the human heart,
but even so, people cannot see the whole scope
of God's work from beginning to end.
So I concluded
there is nothing better than to be happy
and enjoy ourselves as long as we can.
And people should eat and drink
and enjoy the fruits of their labor,
for these are gifts from God.
(Eccles. 3:9-13)

## GOD (LORD, ALMIGHTY)

"But how can a person
be declared innocent in God's sight?
If someone wanted to take God to court,
would it be possible to answer him
even once in a thousand times?
For God is so wise and so mighty.
Who has ever challenged him successfully?"
(Job 9:2-4)

"If only I knew where to find God,
I would go to his court.
I would lay out my case
and present my arguments.
Then I would listen to his reply
and understand what he says to me.
Would he use his great power to argue with me?
No, he would give me a fair hearing.
Honest people can reason with him,
so I would be forever acquitted by my judge.
I go east, but he is not there.
I go west, but I cannot find him.
I do not see him in the north, for he is hidden.
I look to the south, but he is concealed.
But he knows where I am going.
And when he tests me,
I will come out as pure gold."
(Job 23:3-10)

"Why doesn't the Almighty
bring the wicked to judgment?
Why must the godly wait for him in vain?"
(Job 24:1)

"For God speaks again and again,
though people do not recognize it.
He speaks in dreams, in visions of the night,
when deep sleep falls on people
as they lie in their beds.
He whispers in their ears
and terrifies them with warnings.
He makes them turn from doing wrong;
he keeps them from pride." (Elihu)
(Job 33:14-17)

"Listen to me, you who have understanding.
Everyone knows that God doesn't sin!
The Almighty can do no wrong.
He repays people according to their deeds.
He treats people as they deserve.
Truly, God will not do wrong.
The Almighty will not twist justice." (Elihu)
(Job 34:10-12)

"He doesn't care how great a person may be,
and he pays no more attention
to the rich than to the poor.
He made them all." (Elihu)
(Job 34:19)

"We cannot imagine the power of the Almighty;
but even though he is just and righteous,
he does not destroy us.
No wonder people everywhere fear him?
All who are wise show him reverence."(Elihu)
(Job 37:23-24)

God is my shield,
saving those whose hearts are true and right.
(Psalm 7:10)

O Lord, our Lord,
your majestic name fills the earth!
Your glory is higher than the heavens.
(Psalm 8:1)

The Lord is a shelter for the oppressed,
a refuge in times of trouble.
(Psalm 9:9)

But the Lord is in his holy Temple;
the Lord still rules from heaven.
He watches everyone closely,
examining every person on earth.
The Lord examines
both the righteous and the wicked.
He hates those who love violence.
(Psalm 11:4-5)

For the righteous Lord loves justice.
The virtuous will see his face.
(Psalm 11:7)

I will sing to the Lord
because he is good to me.
(Psalm 13:6)

I know the Lord is always with me.
I will not be shaken,
for he is right beside me.
(Psalm 16:8)

I love you, Lord;
you are my strength.
(Psalm 18:1)

God's way is perfect.
All the Lord's promises prove true.
He is a shield
for all who look to him for protection.
For who is God except the Lord?
Who but our God is a solid rock?
(Psalm 18:30-31)

The Lord lives! Praise to my Rock!
May the God of my salvation be exalted!
(Psalm 18:46)

The heavens proclaim the glory of God.
The skies display his craftsmanship.
Day after day they continue to speak;
night after night they make him known.
They speak without a sound or word;
their voice is never heard.
Yet their message has gone throughout the earth,
and their words to all the world.
(Psalm 19:1-4)

Rise up, O Lord, in all your power.
With music and singing
we celebrate your mighty acts.
(Psalm 21:13)

The Lord says, "I will guide you
along the best pathway for your life;
I will advise you and watch over you."
(Psalm 32:8)

The Lord merely spoke,
and the heavens were created.
He breathed the word,
and all the stars were born.
(Psalm 33:6)

The Lord frustrates the plans of the nations
and thwarts all their schemes.
But the Lord's plans stand firm forever;
his intentions can never be shaken.
(Psalm 33:10-11)

But the Lord watches over those who fear him,
those who rely on his unfailing love.
(Psalm 33:18)

The eyes of the Lord,
watch over those who do right;
his ears are open to their cries for help.
(Psalm 34:15)

O Lord my God,
you have performed many wonders for us.
Your plans for us are too numerous to list.
You have no equal.
If I tried to recite all your wonderful deeds,
I would never come to the end of them.
(Psalm 40:5)

Praise the Lord, the God of Israel,
who lives from everlasting to everlasting.
Amen and Amen!
(Psalm 41:13)

God is our refuge and strength,
always ready to help in times of trouble.
So we will not fear when earthquakes come
and the mountains crumble into the sea.
(Psalm 46:1-2)

You are my strength;
I wait for you to rescue me,
for you, O God, are my fortress.
(Psalm 59:9)

I wait quietly before God,
for my victory comes from him.
(Psalm 62:1)

God has spoken plainly,
and I have heard it many times.
Power, O God, belongs to you.
(Psalm 62:11)

Come and see what our God has done,
what awesome miracles he performs for people!
(Psalm 66:5)

May God be merciful and bless us.
May his face smile with favor on us.
(Psalm 67:1)

Father to the fatherless, defender of widows—
this is God, whose dwelling is holy.
God places the lonely in families;
he sets the prisoners free and gives them joy.
But he makes the rebellious
live in a sun-scorched land.
(Psalm 68:5-6)

Our God is a God who saves!
The Sovereign Lord rescues us from death.
(Psalm 68:20)

Summon your might, O God.
Display your power, O God,
as you have in the past.
(Psalm 68:28)

O God, your ways are holy.
Is there any god as mighty as you?
(Psalm 77:13)

For you are great and perform wonderful deeds.
You alone are God.
(Psalm 86:10)

The heavens are yours,
and the earth is yours;
everything in the world is yours—
you created it all.
(Psalm 89:11)

Before the mountains were born,
before you gave birth to the earth and world,
from beginning to end,
you are God.
(Psalm 90:2)

O Lord, what great works you do!
And how deep are your thoughts.
(Psalm 92:5)

Your throne, O Lord,
has stood from time immemorial.
You yourself are from the everlasting past.
(Psalm 93:2)

For the Lord is good.
His unfailing love continues forever,
and his faithfulness continues to each generation.
(Psalm 100:5)

But the love of the Lord remains forever
with those who fear him.
(Psalm 103:17)

Praise the Lord,
everything he has created,
everything in all his kingdom.
Let all that I am praise the Lord.
(Psalm 103:22)

Give thanks to the Lord
and proclaim his greatness.
Let the whole world know what he has done.
(Psalm 105:1)

He is the Lord our God.
His justice is seen throughout the land.
(Psalm 105:7)

The Lord protects those of childlike faith;
I was facing death, and he saved me.
(Psalm 116:6)

The Lord is my strength and my song;
he has given me victory.
(Psalm 118:14)

For your Kingdom is an everlasting Kingdom.
You rule throughout all generations.
The Lord always keeps his promises;
he is gracious in all he does.
(Psalm 145:13)

The Lord is righteous in everything he does;
he is filled with kindness.
The Lord is close to all who call on him,
yes, to all who call on him in truth.
(Psalm 145:17-18)

For the Lord delights in his people;
he crowns the humble with victory.
(Psalm 149:4)

For the Lord grants wisdom!
From his mouth come knowledge and understanding.
(Prov. 2:6)

By wisdom the Lord founded the earth;
by understanding he created the heavens.
(Prov. 3:19)

You need not be afraid of sudden disaster
or the destruction
that comes upon the wicked,
for the Lord is your security.
(Prov. 3:25-26)

For the Lord sees clearly what a man does,
examining every path he takes.
(Prov. 5:21)

The way of the Lord is a stronghold
to those with integrity,
but it destroys the wicked.
(Prov. 10:29)

The Lord detests the way of the wicked,
but he loves those who pursue godliness.
(Prov. 15:9)

The Lord detests evil plans,
but he delights in pure words.
(Prov. 15:26)

No human wisdom or understanding or plan
can stand against the Lord.
(Prov. 21:30)

The rich and poor have this in common:
the Lord made them both.
(Prov. 22:2)

And I know that whatever God does is final.
Nothing can be added to it or taken from it.
God's purpose is that people should fear him.
What is happening now has happened before,
and what will happen in the future
has happened before,
because God makes the same things happen
over and over again.
(Eccles. 3:14-15)

## GODLESS

"The same happens to all who forget God.
The hopes of the godless evaporate.
Their confidence hangs by a thread.
They are leaning on a spider's web.
They cling to their home for security,
but it won't last.
They try to hold it tight,
but it will not endure.
The godless seem like a lush plant,
growing in the sunshine,
its branches spreading across the garden.
Its roots grow down through a pile of stones;
it takes hold on a bed of rocks.
But when it is uprooted,
it's as though it never existed!
That's the end of its life,
and others spring up
from the earth to replace it."(Bildad)
(Job 8:13-19)

"Don't you realize
that from the beginning of time,
ever since people were first placed on the earth,
the triumph of the wicked
has been short lived
and the joy of the godless
has been only temporary?"(Zophar)
(Job 20:4-5)

# GODLY

For the Lord watches over the path of the godly,
but the path of the wicked leads to destruction.
(Psalm 1:6)

You can be sure of this:
the Lord set apart the godly for himself.
The Lord will answer when I call to him.
(Psalm 4:3)

For you bless the godly, Lord;
you surround them with your shield of love.
(Psalm 5:12)

Help, O Lord, for the godly are fast disappearing!
The faithful have vanished from the earth!
Neighbors lie to each other,
speaking with flattering lips and deceitful hearts.
(Psalm 12:1-2)

The godly people in the land
are my true heroes!
I take pleasure in them!
(Psalm 16:3)

Sing to the Lord all you godly ones!
Praise his holy name.
For his anger lasts only a moment,
but his favor lasts a lifetime!
Weeping may last through the night,
but joy comes with the morning.
(Psalm 30:4-5)

It is better to be godly and have little
than to be evil and rich.
For the strength of the wicked will be shattered,
but the Lord takes care of the godly.
(Psalm 37:16-17)

The wicked borrow and never repay,
but the godly are generous givers.
(Psalm 37:21)

The Lord directs the steps of the godly.
He delights in every detail of their lives.
Though they stumble, they will never fall,
for the Lord holds them by the hand.
Once I was young, and now I am old.
Yet I have never seen the godly abandoned
or their children begging for bread.
The godly always give generous loans to others,
and their children are a blessing.
(Psalm 37:23-26)

The Lord rescues the godly;
he is their fortress in times of trouble.
(Psalm 37:39)

Give your burdens to the Lord,
and he will take care of you.
He will not permit the godly to slip and fall.
(Psalm 55:22)

The godly will rejoice in the Lord
and find shelter in him.
And those who do what is right
will praise him.
(Psalm 64:10)

But the godly will flourish like palm trees
and grow strong like cedars of Lebanon.
(Psalm 92:12)

Light shines in the darkness for the godly.
They are generous, compassionate and righteous.
(Psalm 112:4)

The Lord opens the eyes of the blind.
The Lord lifts up
those who are weighed down.
The Lord loves the godly.
(Psalm 146:8)

The Lord will not let the godly go hungry,
but he refuses to satisfy
the craving of the wicked.
(Prov. 10:3)

The words of the godly
are a life-giving fountain;
the words of the wicked
conceal violent intentions.
(Prov. 10:11)

The words of the godly encourage many;
but fools are destroyed
by their lack of common sense.
(Prov. 10:21)

The hopes of the godly result in happiness,
but the expectations of the wicked
come to nothing.
(Prov. 10:28)

The godly are directed by honesty;
the wicked fall beneath their load of sin.
(Prov. 11:5)

Wickedness never brings stability,
but the godly have deep roots.
(Prov. 12:3)

The way of the godly leads to life;
that path does not lead to death.
(Prov. 12:28)

The godly hate lies;
the wicked cause shame and disgrace.
(Prov. 13:5)

The name of the Lord is a strong fortress;
the godly run to him and are safe.
(Prov. 18:10)

The godly may trip seven times,
but they will get up again.
But one disaster is enough
to overthrow the wicked.
(Prov. 24:16)

When the godly succeed everyone is glad.
When the wicked take charge
people go into hiding.
(Prov. 28:12)

## GOOD (GOODNESS)

His wife said to him,
"Are you still trying to maintain your integrity?
Curse God and die."
But Job replied,
"You talk like a foolish woman.
Should we accept only good things
from the hand of God and never anything bad?"
So in all this, Job said nothing wrong.
(Job 2:9-10)

Only fools say in their hearts,
"There is no God."
They are corrupt, and their actions are evil;
not one of them does good!
The Lord looks down from heaven
on the entire human race;
he looks to see if anyone is truly wise,
if anyone seeks God.
But no, all have turned away;
all have become corrupt.
No one does good, not a single one!
(Psalm 14:1-3;53:1-3)

I said to the Lord, "You are my Master!
Every good thing I have comes from you."
(Psalm 16:2)

The Lord is good and does what is right;
he shows the proper path
to those who go astray.
(Psalm 25:8)

Yet I am confident I will see
the Lord's goodness
while I am here in the land of the living.
(Psalm 27:13)

How great is the goodness
you have stored up for those who fear you.
You lavish it on those
who come to you for protection,
blessing them before the watching world.
(Psalm 31:19)

He loves whatever is just and good,
the unfailing love of the Lord fills the earth.
(Psalm 33:5)

Taste and see that the Lord is good.
Oh, the joys of those who take refuge in him!
(Psalm 34:8)

Trust in the Lord and do good.
Then you will live safely in the land and prosper.
(Psalm 37:3)

O Lord, do good to those who are good,
whose hearts are in tune with you.
(Psalm 125:4)

The Lord is good to everyone.
He shows compassion on all his creation.
(Psalm 145:9)

Do not withhold good from those who deserve it
when it's in your power to help them.
If you can help your neighbor now, don't say
"Come back tomorrow, and then I'll help you."
Don't plot harm against your neighbor,
for those who live nearby trust you.
(Prov. 3:27-29)

The godliness of good people rescues them;
the ambition of treacherous people traps them.
(Prov. 11:6)

If you search for good, you will find favor;
but if you search for evil it will find you.
(Prov. 11:27)

The Lord approves of those who are good,
but he condemns those who plan wickedness.
(Prov. 12:2)

Not a single person on earth
is always good and never sins.
(Eccles. 7:20)

In this life, good people are often treated
as though they were wicked
and wicked people are often treated
as though they were good.
This is so meaningless!
(Eccles. 8:14)

## GOSSIP

A gossip goes around telling secrets,
but those who are trustworthy can keep a confidence.
(Prov. 11:13)

A troublemaker plants seeds of strife;
gossip separates the best of friends.
(Prov. 16:28)

A gossip goes around telling secrets,
so don't hang around with chatterers.
(Prov. 20:19)

Fire goes out without wood,
and quarrels disappear when gossip stops.
(Prov.26:20)

## GREAT

O Lord, what great works you do!
And how deep are your thoughts.
(Psalm 92:5)

For the Lord is a great God,
a great King above all gods.
(Psalm 95:3)

O Lord my God, how great you are!
You are robed with honor and majesty.
(Psalm 104:1)

Though the Lord is great,
he cares for the humble,
but keeps his distance from the proud.
(Psalm 138:6)

Great is the Lord!
He is most worthy of praise!
No one can measure his greatness.
(Psalm 145:3)

## GREED ( GREEDY )

Greed brings grief to the whole family,
but those who hate bribes will live.
(Prov. 15:27)

Greedy people try to get rich quick
but don't realize they're headed for poverty.
(Prov. 28:22)

Greed causes fighting;
trusting the Lord leads to prosperity.
(Prov. 28:25)

## GUILT ( GUILTY )

"Although you know I am not guilty,
no one can rescue me from your hands."
(Job 10:7)

Keep your servant from deliberate sins!
Don't let them control me.
Then I will be free of guilt
and innocent of great sin.
(Psalm 19:13)

Yes, what joy for those whose record
the Lord has cleared of guilt,
whose lives are lived in complete honesty!
(Psalm 32:2)

Fools make fun of guilt,
but the godly acknowledge it
and seek reconciliation.
(Prov. 14:9)

Acquitting the guilty and condemning the innocent—
both are detestable to the Lord.
(Prov. 17:15)

The guilty walk a crooked path;
the innocent travel a straight road.
(Prov. 21:8)

# Chapter 11

# H

## HAPPY (HAPPINESS)

Make me walk along the path of your commands,
for that is where my happiness is found.
(Psalm 119:35)

What do people really get for all their hard work?
I have seen the burden God has placed on us all.
Yet God has made everything beautiful
for its own time.
He has planted eternity in the human heart,
but even so, people cannot see
the whole scope of God's work
from beginning to end.
So I concluded
there is nothing better than to be happy
and enjoy ourselves as long as we can.
And people should eat and drink
and enjoy the fruits of their labor,
for these are gifts from God.
(Eccles. 3:9-13)

I also thought about the human condition—
how God proves to people
that they are like animals.
For people and animals share the same fate—
both breathe and both must die.
So people have no real advantage
over the animals.
How meaningless!
Both go to the same place—
they came from dust and they return to dust.
For who can prove
that the human spirit goes up
and the spirit of animals
goes down into the earth?
So I saw that there is nothing better for people
than to be happy in their work.
That is why we are here!
No one will bring us back from death
to enjoy life after we die.
(Eccles. 3:18-22)

## HARD TIMES

People can never predict
when hard times might come.
Like fish in a net or birds in a trap,
people are caught by sudden tragedy.
(Eccles.9:12)

## HARM

Don't pick a fight without reason,
when no one has done you harm.
(Prov. 3:30)

No harm comes to the godly,
but the wicked have their fill of trouble.
(Prov. 12:21)

## HARMONY

How wonderful and pleasant it is
when brothers live together in harmony.
(Psalm 133:1)

## HATE ( HATRED )

O God, you take no pleasure in wickedness;
you cannot tolerate the sins of the wicked.
Therefore, the proud may not stand
in your presence,
for you hate all who do evil.
(Psalm 5:4-5)

They(wicked) repay evil for good
and hatred for love.
(Psalm 109:5)

I hate those with divided loyalties,
but I love your instructions.
(Psalm 119:113)

I hate and abhor all falsehood,
but I love your instructions.
(Psalm 119:163)

There are six things the Lord hates—
no, seven things he detests:
haughty eyes,
a lying tongue,
hands that kill the innocent,
a heart that plots evil,
feet that race to do wrong,
a false witness who pours out lies,
a person who sows discord in a family.
(Prov. 6:16-19)

Hatred stirs up quarrels,
but love makes up for all offenses.
(Prov. 10:12)

Hiding hatred makes you a liar;
slandering others makes you a fool.(Prov.10:18)

## HEART(S)

End the evil of those who are wicked,
and defend the righteous.
For you look deep within the mind and heart,
O righteous God.
God is my shield,
saving those whose hearts are true and right.
(Psalm 7:9-10)

I will praise you, Lord, with all my heart.
I will tell of all the marvelous things
you have done.
(Psalm 9:1)

O Lord, how long will you forget me?
Forever?
How long will you look the other way?
How long must I struggle
with anguish in my soul,
with sorrow in my heart every day?
How long will my enemy have the upper hand?
(Psalm 13:1-2)

Who may worship in your sanctuary, Lord?
Who may enter your presence
on your holy hill?
Those who lead blameless lives
and do what is right,
speaking the truth from sincere hearts.
(Psalm 15:1-2)

The commandments of the Lord are right,
bringing joy to the heart.
The commands of the Lord are clear,
giving insight for living.
(Psalm 19:8)

May the words of my mouth
and the meditation of my heart
be pleasing to you,
O Lord, my rock and my redeemer.
(Psalm 19:14)

May he grant your heart's desires
and make all your plans succeed.
(Psalm 20:4)

Put me on trial, Lord,
and cross-examine me.
Test my motives and my heart.
(Psalm 26:2)

Though a mighty army surrounds me,
my heart will not be afraid.
Even if I am attacked,
I will remain confident.
(Psalm 27:3)

The Lord is my strength and shield.
I trust him with all my heart.
He helps me and my heart is filled with joy.
I burst out in songs of thanksgiving.
(Psalm 28:7)

In him our hearts rejoice,
for we trust in his holy name.
(Psalm 33:21)

Pour out your unfailing love
on those who love you;
give justice to those with honest hearts.
(Psalm 36:10)

I take joy in doing your will, my God,
for your instructions are written on my heart.
(Psalm 40:8)

Create in me a clean heart, O God.
Renew a loyal spirit within me.
(Psalm 51:10)

The sacrifice you desire is a broken spirit.
You will not reject
a broken and repentant heart, O God.
(Psalm 51:17)

Truly God is good to Israel,
to those whose hearts are pure.
(Psalm 73:1)

My health may fail,
and my spirit may grow weak,
but God remains the strength of my heart;
he is mine forever.
(Psalm 73:26)

Teach me your ways, O Lord,
that I may live according to your truth!
Grant me purity of heart,
so that I may honor you.
With all my heart I will praise you,
O Lord, my God.
I will give glory to your name forever.
(Psalm 86:11-12)

Let all that I am praise the Lord;
with my whole heart,
I will praise his holy name.
(Psalm 103:1)

My heart is confident in you, O God;
no wonder I can sing your praises
with all my heart!
(Psalm 108:1)

Joyful are those who obey his laws
and search for him with all their hearts.
(Psalm 119:2)

I have hidden your word in my heart,
that I might not sin against you.
(Psalm 119:11)

Your laws are my treasure;
they are my heart's delight.
(Psalm 119:111)

Powerful people harass me without a cause,
but my heart trembles only at your word.
(Psalm 119:161)

O Lord, you have examined my heart
and know everything about me.
(Psalm 139:1)

Search me, O God, and know my heart;
test me and know my anxious thoughts.
Point out anything in me that offends you,
and lead me along the path of everlasting life.
(Psalm 139:23-24)

Guard your heart above all else,
for it determines the course of your life.
(Prov. 4:23)

Deceit fills hearts that are plotting evil;
joy fills hearts that are planning peace!
(Prov. 12:20)

Each heart knows its own bitterness
and no one else can fully share its joy.
(Prov. 14:10)

For the despondent, every day brings trouble;
for the happy heart, life is a continual feast.
(Prov. 15:15)

The heart of the godly
thinks carefully before speaking;
the mouth of the wicked
overflows with evil words.
(Prov. 15:28)

A cheerful heart is good medicine,
but a broken spirit saps a person's strength.
(Prov. 17:22)

Who can say,
"I have cleansed my heart;
I am pure and free from sin?"
(Prov. 20:9)

People may be right in their own eyes,
but the Lord examines their heart.
(Prov. 21:2)

Whoever loves a pure heart
and gracious speech
will have the king as a friend.
(Prov. 22:11)

Singing cheerful songs
to a person with a heavy heart,
is like taking someone's coat in cold weather
or pouring vinegar in a wound.
(Prov. 25:20)

HONEST ( HONESTY )

He grants a treasure of common sense
to the honest.
He is a shield to those who walk with integrity.
(Prov. 2:7)

Honesty guides good people;
dishonesty destroys treacherous people.
(Prov. 11:3)

An honest answer is like a kiss of friendship.
(Prov. 24:26)

## HONEY

Do you like honey?
Don't eat too much, or it will make you sick!
(Prov. 25:16)

## HOPE

"He rescues the poor
from the cutting words of the strong,
and rescues them
from the clutches of the powerful.
And so at last the poor have hope
and the snapping jaws of the wicked are shut."(Eliphaz)
(Job 5:15-16)

"Having hope will give you courage."(Zophar)
(Job 11:18)

"Can the dead live again?
If so, this would give me hope
through all my years of struggle,
and I would eagerly await the release of death."
(Job 14:14)

"I helped those without hope,
and they blessed me.
And I caused the widows' hearts to sing for joy."
(Job 29:13)

But the needy will not be ignored forever;
the hopes of the poor
will not always be crushed.
(Psalm 9:18)

Lead me by your truth and teach me,
for you are the God who saves me.
All day long I put my hope in you.
(Psalm 25:5)

We put our hope in the Lord.
He is our help and our shield.
(Psalm 33:20)

Put your hope in the Lord
Travel steadily along his path.
(Psalm 37:34)

And so, Lord, where do I put my hope?
My only hope is in you.
(Psalm 39:7)

Why am I discouraged?
Why is my heart so sad?
I will put my hope in God!
I will praise him again—my Savior and my God!
(Psalm 42:5)

You faithfully answer our prayers
with awesome deeds,
O God, our Savior.
You are the hope of everyone on earth,
even those who sail on distant seas.
(Psalm 65:5)

O Lord, you alone are my hope.
I've trusted you, O Lord, from childhood.
(Psalm 71:5)

When doubts filled my mind,
Your comfort gave me renewed hope and cheer.
(Psalm 94:19)

Do not snatch your word of truth from me,
for your regulations are my only hope.
(Psalm 119:43)

May all who fear you find in me
a cause for joy,
for I have put my hope in your word.
(Psalm 119:74)

Lord, sustain me as you promised,
that I may live!
Do not let my hope be crushed.
(Psalm 119:116)

Hope deferred makes the heart sick,
but a dream fulfilled is a tree of life.
(Prov. 13:12)

There is more hope for fools
than for people who think they are wise.
(Prov. 26:12)

There is more hope for a fool
than for someone who speaks without thinking.
(Prov. 29:20)

## HOUSE

I was glad when they said to me,
"Let us go to the house of the Lord."
(Psalm 122:1)

Unless the Lord builds a house,
the work of the builders is wasted.
(Psalm 127:1)

## HUMANITY(HUMAN BEINGS, PEOPLE)

"How frail is humanity!
How short is life, how full of trouble!
We blossom like a flower and then wither.
Like a passing shadow, we quickly disappear."
(Job 14:1)

"And this is what he says to all humanity:
'The fear of the Lord is true wisdom;
to forsake evil is real understanding.'"
(Job 28:28)

When I look at the night sky
and see the work of your fingers—
the moon and the stars you set in place—
what are mere mortals,
that you should think about them,
human beings that you should care for them?
Yet you made them
only a little lower than God
and crowned them with glory and honor.
You gave them charge
over everything you made,
putting all things under their authority.
(Psalm 8:3-6)

The Lord looks down from heaven
on the entire human race;
he looks to see if anyone is truly wise,
if anyone seeks God.
But no, all have turned away;
all have become corrupt.
No one does good, not a single one!
(Psalms 14:2-3;53:2-3)

The earth is the Lord's and everything in it.
The world and all its people belong to him.
(Psalm 24:1)

The Lord looks down from heaven
and sees the whole human race.
From his throne he observes
all who live on the earth.
He made their hearts
so he understands everything they do.
(Psalm 33:13-15)

You care for people and animals alike, O Lord.
How precious is your unfailing love, O God!
All humanity finds shelter
in the shadow of your wings.
(Psalm 36:6-7)

O Lord, what are human beings
that you should notice them,
mere mortals that you should think about them?
For they are like a breath of air;
their days are like a passing shadow.
(Psalm 144:3-4)

## HUMILITY

Pride leads to disgrace,
but with humility comes wisdom.
(Prov. 11:2)

Fear of the Lord teaches wisdom;
humility precedes honor.
(Prov. 15:33)

True humility and fear of the Lord
lead to riches, honor and long life.
(Prov. 22:4)

Pride ends in humiliation
while humility brings honor.
(Prov. 29:23)

# Chapter 12

# I

## IMMORAL

For the lips of an immoral woman
are as sweet as honey,
but in the end she is as bitter as poison,
as dangerous as a double-edged sword.
Her feet go down to death;
her steps lead straight to the grave.
For she cares nothing about the path to life.
She staggers down a crooked trail
and doesn't realize it.
(Prov. 5:3-6)

## INHERITANCE

An inheritance obtained too early in life,
is not a blessing in the end.
(Prov. 20:21)

## INJUSTICE

Those who plant injustice will harvest disaster,
and their reign of terror will come to an end.
(Prov. 22:8)

## INNOCENT (INNOCENCE)

"So who am I, that I should try to answer God
or even reason with him?
Even if I were right,
I would have no defense.
I could only plead for mercy.
And even if I summoned him and he responded,
I'm not sure he would listen to me.
For he attacks me with a storm
and repeatedly wounds me without cause.
He will not let me catch my breath,
but fills me instead with bitter sorrows.
If it's a question of strength,
he's the strong one.
If it's a matter of justice,
who dares to summon him to court?
Though I am innocent,
my own mouth would pronounce me guilty.
Though I am blameless,
it would prove me wicked."
(Job 9:14-20)

"Get rid of your sins
and leave all iniquity behind you.
Then your face will brighten with innocence.
You will be strong and free of fear."(Zophar)
(Job 11:14-15)

"As long as I live, while I have breath from God,
my lips will speak no evil,
and my tongue will speak no lies.
I will never concede that you are right;
I will defend my integrity until I die.
I will maintain my innocence without wavering.
My conscience is clear for as long as I live."
(Job 27:3-6)

Answer me when I call to you,
O God who declares me innocent.
Free me from my troubles.
Have mercy on me—hear my prayer.
(Psalm 4:1)

Those who refuse to gossip
or harm their neighbors
or speak evil of their friends.
Those who despise flagrant sinners,
and honor the faithful followers of the Lord
and keep their promises
even when it hurts.
Those who lend money
without charging interest,
and who cannot be bribed
to lie about the innocent.
Such people will stand firm forever.
(Psalm 15:3-5)

The Lord rewarded me for doing right;
he restored me because of my innocence.
(Psalm 18:20)

Keep your servant from deliberate sins!
Don't let them control me.
Then I will be free of guilt
and innocent of great sin.
(Psalm 19:13)

Declare me innocent, O Lord
for I have acted with integrity.
I have trusted in the Lord without wavering.
(Psalm 26:1)

## INSIGHT

Cry out for insight,
and ask for understanding.
Search for them as you would for silver;
seek them like hidden treasures.
Then you will understand
what it means to fear the Lord,
and you will gain knowledge of God.
(Prov. 2:3-5)

## INSTRUCTIONS

Your instructions are more valuable to me
than millions in gold and silver.
(Psalm 119:72)

Surround me with your tender mercies
so I may live,
for your instructions are my delight.
(Psalm 119:77)

Oh, how I love your instructions!
I think about them all day long.
Your commands make me wiser than my enemies,
for they are my constant guide.
(Psalm 119:97-98)

## INSULT

If you insult your father or mother,
Your light will be snuffed out in total darkness.
(Prov. 20:20)

## INTEGRITY

His wife said to him,
"Are you still trying to maintain your integrity?
Curse God and die."
(Job 2:9)

"But if you pray to God
and seek the favor of the Almighty,
and if you are pure and live with integrity,
he will surely rise up
and restore your happy home.
And though you started with little,
you will end with much."(Bildad)
(Job 8:5-7)

"But look, God will not reject a person of integrity,
nor will he lend a hand to the wicked.
He will once again
fill your mouth with laughter
and your lips with shouts of joy."(Bildad)
(Job 8:20-21)

"As long as I live,
while I have breath from God,
my lips will speak no evil,
and my tongue will speak no lies.
I will never concede that you are right;
I will defend my integrity until I die.
I will maintain my innocence without wavering.
My conscience is clear for as long as I live."
(Job 27:3-6)

"Have I lied to anyone or deceived anyone?
Let God weigh me on the scales of justice,
for he knows my integrity."
(Job 31:5-6)

To the faithful, you show yourself faithful;
to those with integrity, you show integrity.
(Psalm 18:25)

Declare me innocent, O Lord,
for I have acted with integrity.
I have trusted in the Lord without wavering.
(Psalm 26:1)

Joyful are people of integrity,
who follow the instructions of the Lord.
(Psalm 119:1)

He is a shield
to those who walk with integrity.
(Prov. 2:7)

People with integrity walk safely,
but those who follow crooked paths
will slip and fall.
(Prov. 10:9)

The way of the Lord is a stronghold
to those with integrity,
but it destroys the wicked.
(Prov. 10:29)

The Lord detests people with crooked hearts,
but he delights in those with integrity.
(Prov. 11:20)

The godly walk with integrity;
blessed are their children who follow them.
(Prov. 20:7)

# Chapter 13

# J

## JEALOUSY

Anger is cruel, and wrath is like a flood,
but jealousy is even more dangerous.
(Prov. 27:4)

## JOY (JOYFUL)

"But consider the joy of those corrected by God!
Do not despise the discipline of the Almighty
when you sin.
For though he wounds, he also bandages.
He strikes, but his hands also heals."(Eliphaz)
(Job 5:17-18)

Oh, the joys of those
who do not follow the advice of the wicked,
or stand around with sinners,
or join in with mockers.
But they delight in the law of the Lord,
meditating on it day and night.
(Psalm 1:1-2)

But let all who take refuge in you rejoice;
let them sing joyful praises forever.
Spread your protection over them,
that all who love your name
may be filled with joy.
(Psalm 5:11)

The commandments of the Lord are right,
bringing joy to the heart.
The commands of the Lord are clear,
giving insight for living. (Psalm 19:8)
May he grant your heart's desires
and make all your plans succeed.
May we shout for joy
when we hear of your victory
and raise a victory banner
in the name of our God.
May the Lord answer all your prayers.
(Psalm 20:4-5)

The Lord is my strength and shield.
I trust him with all my heart.
He helps me and my heart is filled with joy.
I burst out in songs of thanksgiving.
(Psalm 28:7)

Sing to the Lord, all you godly ones!
Praise his holy name.
For his anger lasts only a moment,
but his favor lasts a lifetime.
Weeping may last through the night,
but joy comes with the morning.
(Psalm 30:4-5)

You have turned my mourning
into joyful dancing.
You have taken away my clothes of mourning
and clothed me with joy,
that I might sing praises to you
and not be silent.
O Lord my God, I will give you thanks forever.
(Psalm 30:11-12)

Yes, what joy for those
whose record the Lord has cleared of guilt,
whose lives are lived in complete honesty!
(Psalm 32:2)

Those who look to him for help
will be radiant with joy;
no shadow of shame will darken their faces.
(Psalm 34:5)

Taste and see that the Lord is good.
Oh, the joys of those who take refuge in him!
(Psalm 34:8)

Oh, the joys of those who trust the Lord,
who have no confidence in the proud
or in those who worship idols.
(Psalm 40:4)

I take joy in doing your will, my God,
for your instructions are written on my heart.
(Psalm 40:8)

Oh, the joys of those who are kind to the poor!
The Lord rescues them
when they are in trouble.
(Psalm 41:1)

The meadows are clothed with flocks of sheep,
and the valleys are carpeted with grain.
They all shout and sing for joy!
(Psalm 65:13)

But may all who search for you
be filled with joy and gladness in you.
(Psalm 70:4)

Joyful indeed are those whose God is the Lord.
(Psalm 144:15)

The life of the godly is full of light and joy,
but the light of the wicked will be snuffed out.
(Prov. 13:9)

Foolishness brings joy to those with no sense;
a sensible person stays on the right path.
(Prov. 15:21)

A cheerful look brings joy to the heart;
good news makes for good health.
(Prov. 15:30)

## JUSTICE (JUST)

"Can any mortal be pure?
Can anyone born of a woman be just?"(Eliphaz)
(Job 15:14)

"Everything I did was honest.
Righteousness covered me like a robe,
and I wore justice like a turban."
(Job 29:14)

"Have I lied to anyone or deceived anyone?
Let God weigh me
on the scales of justice,
for he knows my integrity."
(Job 31:5-6)

"Listen to me, you who have understanding.
Everyone knows that God doesn't sin!
The Almighty can do no wrong.
He repays people according to their deeds.
He treats people as they deserve.
Truly, God will not do wrong.
The Almighty will not twist justice."(Elihu)
(Job 34:10-12)

"We cannot imagine the power of the Almighty;
but even though he is just and righteous,
he does not destroy us.
No wonder people everywhere fear him.
All who are wise show him reverence."(Elihu)
(Job 37:23-24)

Arise, O Lord, in anger!
Stand up against the fury of my enemies!
Wake up, my God, and bring justice!
(Psalm 7:6)

I will thank the Lord because he is just;
I will sing praise
to the name of the Lord Most High.
(Psalm 7:17)

But the Lord reigns forever,
executing judgment from his throne.
He will judge the world with justice
and rule the nations with fairness.
(Psalm 9:7-8)

The Lord is known for his justice.
The wicked are trapped by their own deeds.
(Psalm 9:16)

You will bring justice
to the orphans and the oppressed,
so mere people can no longer terrify them.
(Psalm 10:18)

For the righteous Lord loves justice.
The virtuous will see his face.
(Psalm 11:7)

Your righteousness is like the mighty mountains,
Your justice like the ocean depths.
You care for people and animals alike, O Lord.
(Psalm 36:6)

Pour out your unfailing love
on those who love you;
give justice to those with honest hearts.
(Psalm 36:10)

Commit everything you do to the Lord.
Trust him, and he will help you.
He will make your innocence
radiate like the dawn,
and the justice of your cause
will shine like the noonday sun.
(Psalm 37:5-6)

I will praise your mighty deeds,
O Sovereign Lord.
I will tell everyone that you alone are just.
(Psalm 71:16)

Righteousness and justice
are the foundation of your throne.
Unfailing love and truth
walk before you as attendants.
(Psalm 89:14)

Judgment will again be founded on justice,
and those with virtuous hearts will pursue it.
(Psalm 94:15)

He is coming to judge the earth.
He will judge the world with justice,
and the nations with his truth.
(Psalm 96:13)

The Lord gives righteousness and justice
to all who are treated unfairly.
(Psalm 103:6)

He is the Lord our God.
His justice is seen throughout the land.
(Psalm 105:7)

All he does is just and good,
and all his commandments are trustworthy.
They are forever true,
to be obeyed faithfully and with integrity.
(Psalm 111:7-8)

Don't leave me to the mercy of my enemies,
for I have done what is just and right.
(Psalm119:121)

Your justice is eternal,
and your instructions are perfectly true.
(Psalm 119:142)

For the Lord will give justice to his people
and have compassion on his servants.
(Psalm 135:14)

He gives justice to the oppressed
and food to the hungry.
The Lord frees the prisoners.
(Psalm 146:7)

He guards the paths of the just
and protects those who are faithful to him.
(Prov. 2:8)

The plans of the godly are just;
the advice of the wicked is treacherous.
(Prov. 12:5)

The wicked take secret bribes
to pervert the course of justice.
(Prov. 17:23)

It is not right to acquit the guilty
or deny justice to the innocent.
(Prov. 18:5)

A corrupt witness makes a mockery of justice;
the mouth of the wicked gulps down evil.
(Prov. 19:28)

The Lord is more pleased
when we do what is right and just
than when we offer him sacrifices.
(Prov. 21:3)

Speak up for those
who cannot speak for themselves;
ensure justice for those being crushed.
Yes, speak up for the poor and helpless,
and see that they get justice.
(Prov. 31:8-9)

# Chapter 14

# K

## KIND (KINDNESS)

Never let loyalty and kindness leave you!
Tie them around your neck as a reminder.
Write them deep within your heart.
Then you will find favor
with both God and people,
and you will earn a good reputation.
(Prov. 3:3-4)

Your kindness will reward you,
but your cruelty will destroy you.
(Prov. 11:17)

Kind words are like honey—
sweet to the soul and healthy for the body.
(Prov. 16:24)

## KNOW (KNOWLEDGE)

"Can you solve the mysteries of God?
Can you discover everything about the Almighty?
Such knowledge is higher than the heavens."(Zophar)
(Job 11:7-8)

Be still and know that I am God!
I will be honored by every nation.
I will be honored throughout the world.
(Psalm 46:10)

The Lord knows people's thoughts;
he knows they are worthless!
(Psalm 94:11)

For he knows how weak we are;
he remembers we are only dust.
(Psalm 103:14)

Keep me from lying to myself;
give me the privilege
of knowing your instructions.
(Psalm 119:29)

Let me be united with all who fear you,
with those who know your laws.
(Psalm 119:79)

Yes, I obey your commandments and laws
because you know everything I do.
(Psalm 119:168)

O Lord, you have examined my heart
and know everything about me.
You know when I sit down or stand up.
You know my thoughts even when I'm far away.
You see me when I travel
and when I rest at home.
You know everything I do.
You know what I am going to say
even before I say it, Lord.
You go before me and follow me.
You place your hand of blessing on my head.
Such knowledge is too wonderful for me,
too great for me to understand!
(Psalm 139:1-6)

When they cry for help,
I will not answer.
Though they anxiously search for me,
they will not find me.
For they hated knowledge
and chose not to fear the Lord.
(Prov. 1:28-29)

Choose my instruction rather than silver,
and knowledge rather than pure gold.
(Prov. 8:10)

Fear of the Lord
is the foundation of wisdom.
Knowledge of the Holy One
results in good judgment.
(Prov. 9:10)

Wise people treasure knowledge,
but the babbling of a fool invites disaster.
(Prov. 10:14)

The wise don't make a show of their knowledge,
but fools broadcast their foolishness.
(Prov. 12:23)

A wise person is hungry for knowledge,
while the fool feeds on trash.
(Prov. 15:14)

Intelligent people are always ready to learn.
Their ears are open for knowledge.
(Prov. 18:15)

Enthusiasm without knowledge is no good;
haste makes mistakes.
(Prov. 19:2)

If you stop listening to instruction, my child,
you will turn your back on knowledge.
(Prov. 19:27)

The Lord preserves those with knowledge,
but he ruins the plans of the treacherous.
(Prov. 22:12)

The greater my wisdom,
the greater my grief.
To increase knowledge only increases sorrow.
(Eccles. 1:18)

Some people work wisely with knowledge and skill,
then must leave the fruit of their efforts
to someone who hasn't worked for it.
(Eccles. 2:21)

God gives wisdom, knowledge and joy
to those who please him.
(Eccles. 2:26)

Divide your investments among many places,
for you do not know what risks might lie ahead.
(Eccles. 11:2)

Plant your seed in the morning
and keep busy all afternoon,
for you do not know if profit will come
from one activity or another—or maybe both.
(Eccles. 11:6)

# Chapter 15

# L

## LAUGHTER

Laughter can conceal a heavy heart,
but when the laughter ends, the grief remains.
(Prov. 14:13)

## LAZY

Lazy people irritate their employers,
like vinegar to the teeth or smoke to the eyes.
(Prov. 10:26)

Work hard and become a leader;
be lazy and become a slave.
(Prov. 12:24)

Lazy people want much but get little,
but those who work hard will prosper.
(Prov. 13:4)

A lazy person's way is blocked with briers,
but the path of the upright is an open highway.
(Prov. 15:19)

A lazy person is as bad as someone who destroys things.
(Prov. 18:9)

Lazy people sleep soundly,
but idleness leaves them hungry.
(Prov. 19:15)

Despite their desires,
the lazy will come to ruin,
for their hands refuse to work.
(Prov. 21:25)

## LIFE (LIVE)

"But I don't have the strength to endure.
I have nothing to live for."
(Job 6:11)

"I am disgusted with my life.
Let me complain freely.
I will speak in the bitterness of my soul.
I will say to God,
'Don't simply condemn me—
tell me the charge you are bringing against me.'"
(Job 10:1-2)

"You guided my conception
and formed me in the womb.
You clothe me with skin and flesh
and you knit my bones and sinews together.
You gave me life
and showed me your unfailing love.
My life was preserved by your care."
(Job 10:10-12)

"For the life of every living thing is in his hand,
and the breath of every human being."
(Job 12:10)

"How frail is humanity!
How short is life, how full of trouble!
We blossom like a flower and then wither.
Like a passing shadow, we quickly disappear."
(Job 14:1)

The one thing I ask of the Lord—
the thing I seek most—
is to live in the house of the Lord
all the days of my life,
delighting in the Lord's perfections
and meditating in his Temple.
(Psalm 27:4)

For you are the fountain of life,
the light by which we see.
(Psalm 36:9)

Teach us to realize the brevity of life,
so that we may grow in wisdom.
(Psalm 90:12)

Those who live in the shelter of the Most High
will find rest in the shadow of the Almighty.
(Psalm 91:1)

He fills my life with good things.
My youth is renewed like the eagle's!
(Psalm 103:5)

Turn my eyes from worthless things,
and give me life through your word.
(Psalm 119:37)

This is how I spend my life;
obeying your commandments.
(Psalm 119:56)

I pondered the direction of my life,
and I turned to follow your laws.
(Psalm 119:59)

I will never forget your commandments,
for by them you give me life.
(Psalm 119:93)
My life constantly hangs in the balance,
but I will not stop obeying your instructions.
(Psalm 119:109)

You watched me
as I was being formed in utter seclusion,
as I was woven together
in the dark of the womb.
You saw me before I was born.
Every day of my life
was recorded in your book.
Every moment was laid out
before a single day had passed.
(Psalm 139:15-16)

These are the proverbs of Solomon,
David's son, king of Israel.
Their purpose is to teach people
wisdom and discipline,
to help them understand the insights of the wise.
Their purpose is to teach people to live
disciplined and successful lives,
to help them do what is right, just and fair.
(Prov. 1:1-3)

Such is the fate of all
who are greedy for money;
it robs them of life.
(Prov. 1:19)

My child,
never forget the things I have taught you.
Store my commands in your heart.
If you do this, you will live many years,
and your life will be satisfying.
(Prov. 3:1-2)

Wisdom is more precious than rubies;
nothing you desire can compare with her.
She offers you long life in her right hand,
and riches and honor in her left.
(Prov. 3:15-16)

Wisdom is a tree of life
to those who embrace her;
happy are those who hold her tightly.
(Prov. 3:18)

My father taught me,
"Take my words to heart.
Follow my commands and you will live."
(Prov. 4:4)

My child,
listen to me and do as I say,
and you will have a long, good life.
(Prov. 4:10)

Take hold of my instructions;
don't let them go.
Guard them, for they are the key to life.
(Prov. 4:13)

"I Wisdom live together with good judgment.
I know where to discover
knowledge and discernment."
(Prov. 8:12)

For whoever finds me(wisdom) finds life
and receives favor from the Lord.
(Prov. 8:35)

Wisdom will multiply your days
and add years to your life.
(Prov. 9:11)

Tainted wealth has no lasting value
but right living can save your life.
(Prov. 10:2)

The earnings of the godly enhance their lives,
but evil people squander their money on sin.
(Prov. 10:16)

Godly people find life;
evil people find death.
(Prov. 11:19)

The seeds of good deeds become a tree of life;
a wise person wins friends.
(Prov. 11:30)

The way of the godly leads to life;
that path does not lead to death.
(Prov. 12:28)

Those who control their tongue
will have a long life;
opening your mouth can ruin everything.
(Prov. 13:3)

Hope deferred makes the heart sick,
but a dream fulfilled is a tree of life.
(Prov. 13:12)

Gentle words are a tree of life;
a deceitful tongue crushes the spirit.
(Prov. 15:4)

For the despondent,
every day brings trouble;
for the happy heart,
life is a continual feast.
(Prov. 15:15)

When people's lives please the Lord,
even their enemies are at peace with them.
(Prov. 16:7)

Corrupt people walk a thorny, treacherous road;
whoever values life will avoid it.
(Prov. 22:5)

I said to myself,
"Come on, let's try pleasure.
Let's look for the good things in life."
But I found that this, too, was meaningless.
(Eccles. 2:1)

So I came to hate life
because everything done here under the sun
is so troubling.
Everything is meaningless—
like chasing the wind.
(Eccles. 2:17)

So what do people get in this life
for all their hard work and anxiety?
Their days of labor
are filled with pain and grief;
even at night their minds cannot rest.
It is all meaningless.
(Eccles. 2:22-23)

So I saw that there is nothing better for people
than to be happy in their work.
That is why we are here!
No one will bring us back from death
to enjoy life after we die.
(Eccles. 3:22)

Wisdom and money
can get you almost anything,
but only wisdom can save your life.
(Eccles. 7:12)

## LIGHT

"Surely the light of the wicked will be snuffed out.
The sparks of their fire will not glow.
The light in their tent will grow dark.
The lamp hanging above them
will be quenched."(Bildad)
(Job 18:5-6)

"You will succeed
in whatever you choose to do,
and the light will shine
on the road ahead of you."(Eliphaz)
(Job 22:28)

"Thieves break into houses at night
and sleep in the daytime.
They are not acquainted with the light.
The black night is their morning.
They ally themselves
with the terrors of darkness."
(Job 24:16-17)

The Lord is my light and my salvation—
so why should I be afraid?
The Lord is my fortress,
protecting me from danger,
so why should I tremble?
(Psalm 27:1)

Light shines on the godly
and joy on those whose hearts are right.
(Psalm 97:11)

Your word is a lamp to guide my feet
and a light for my path.
(Psalm 119:105)

The teaching of your word gives light,
so even the simple can understand.
(Psalm 119:130)

## LISTEN

"Listen to my charge;
pay attention to my arguments."
(Job 13:6)

"Listen closely to what I am saying.
That's one consolation you can give me."
(Job 21:2)

"But it is wrong to say God doesn't listen,
to say the Almighty isn't concerned."(Elihu)
(Job 35:13)

Listen to my cry for help, my King and my God,
for I pray to no one but you.
Listen to my voice in the morning, Lord.
Each morning I bring my requests to you
and wait expectantly.
(Psalm 5:2-3)

I am praying to you
because I know you will answer, O God.
Bend down and listen as I pray.
(Psalm 17:6)

For he has not ignored or belittled
the suffering of the needy.
He has not turned his back on them,
but has listened to their cries for help.
(Psalm 22:24)

Hear my prayer, O Lord!
Listen to my cries for help!
Don't ignore my tears.
(Psalm 39:12)

Listen to my prayer, O God.
Do not ignore my cry for help!
Please listen and answer me,
for I am overwhelmed by my troubles.
(Psalm 55:1-2)

They(wicked) spit venom like deadly snakes;
they are like cobras that refuse to listen.
(Psalm 58:4)

If I had not confessed the sin in my heart,
the Lord would not have listened.
But God did listen!
He paid attention to my prayer.
(Psalm 66:18-19)

"Oh, that my people would listen to me!
Oh, that Israel would follow me,
walking in my paths!"
(Psalm 81:13)

I listen carefully
to what God the Lord is saying,
for he speaks peace to his faithful people.
But let them not return
to their foolish ways.
(Psalm 85:8)

He will listen to the prayers of the destitute.
He will not reject their pleas.
(Psalm 102:17)

Let the wise listen to these proverbs
and become even wiser.
(Prov. 1:5)

Listen as Wisdom calls out!
Hear as understanding raises her voice!
(Prov. 8:1)

And so, my children, listen to me(Wisdom),
for all who follow my ways are joyful.
Listen to my instruction and be wise.
Don't ignore it.
(Prov. 8:32-33)

If you listen to constructive criticism,
you will be at home among the wise.
If you reject discipline,
you only harm yourself;
but if you listen to correction,
you grow in understanding.
(Prov. 15:31-32)

Those who listen to instruction will prosper;
those who trust the Lord will be joyful.
(Prov. 16:20)

Wrongdoers eagerly listen to gossip;
liars pay close attention to slander.
(Prov. 17:4)

Spouting off before listening to the facts
is both shameful and foolish.
(Prov. 18:13)

Commit yourself to instruction;
listen carefully to words of knowledge.
(Prov. 23:12)

My child, listen and be wise:
keep your heart on the right course.
(Prov. 23:19)

To one who listens,
valid criticism is like a gold earing
or other gold jewelry.
(Prov. 25:12)

## LOVE

"You guided my conception
and formed me in the womb.
You clothed me with skin and flesh,
and you knit my bones and sinews together.
You gave me life
and showed me your unfailing love.
My life was preserved by your care."
(Job 10:10-12)

"My close friends detests me.
Those I loved have turned against me.'
(Job 19:19)

"He makes these things happen,
either to punish people
or to show his unfailing love."
(Job 37:13)

Because of your unfailing love,
I can enter your house;
I will worship at your Temple with deepest awe.
(Psalm 5:7)

For you bless the godly, O Lord,
you surround them
with your shield of love.
(Psalm 5:12)

Return, O Lord, and rescue me.
Save me because of your unfailing love.
For the dead do not remember you.
Who can praise you from the grave?
(Psalm 6:4-5)

But I trust in your unfailing love.
I will rejoice
because you have rescued me.
I will sing to the Lord,
because he is good to me.
(Psalm 13:5-6)

For the king trusts in the Lord.
The unfailing love of the Most High
will keep him from stumbling.
(Psalm 21:7)

Surely, your goodness and unfailing love
will pursue me all the days of my life,
and I will live
in the house of the Lord forever.
(Psalm 23:6)

Remember, O Lord,
your compassion and unfailing love,
which you have shown from long ages past.
(Psalm 25:6)

The Lord leads with unfailing love and faithfulness,
all who keep his covenant and obey his demands.
(Psalm 25:10)

Put me on trial, Lord,
and cross-examine me.
Test my motives and my heart.
For I am always aware of your unfailing love,
and I have lived according to your truth.
(Psalm 26:2-3)

I love your sanctuary, Lord,
the place where your glorious presence dwells.
(Psalm 26:8)

I will be glad
and rejoice in your unfailing love,
for you have seen my troubles,
and you care about
the anguish in my soul.
(Psalm 31:7)

Praise the Lord,
for he has shown me
the wonders of his unfailing love.
(Psalm 31:21)

Love the Lord, all you godly ones!
For the Lord protects
those who are loyal to him,
but he harshly punishes the arrogant.
(Psalm 31:23)

Many sorrows come to the wicked,
but unfailing love
surrounds those who trust the Lord.
(Psalm 32:10)

He loves whatever is just and good;
the unfailing love of the Lord fills the earth.
(Psalm 33:5)

Let your unfailing love surround us, Lord,
for our hope is in you alone.
(Psalm 33:22)

Your unfailing love, O Lord,
is as vast as the heavens;
your faithfulness reaches beyond the clouds.
(Psalm 36:5)

Lord, don't hold back
your tender mercies from me.
Let your unfailing love and faithfulness
always protect me.
(Psalm 40:11)

O God,
we meditate on your unfailing love
as we worship in your Temple.
(Psalm 48:9)

Unfailing love and truth have met together.
Righteousness and peace have kissed.
(Psalm 85:10)

O Lord, you are so good,
so ready to forgive,
so full of unfailing love
for all who ask for your help.
(Psalm 86:5)

I will sing of the Lord's unfailing love forever!
Young and old will hear of your faithfulness.
Your unfailing love will last forever.
Your faithfulness is as enduring as the heavens.
(Psalm 89:1-2)

Righteousness and justice
are the foundation of your throne.
Unfailing love and truth
walk before you as attendants.
(Psalm 89:14)

For his unfailing love
toward those who fear him is as great
as the height of the heavens above the earth.
(Psalm 103:11)

Give thanks to the Lord,
for he is good!
His faithful love endures forever.
(Psalm 106:1)

Give me an eagerness for your laws
rather than a love for money.
(Psalm 119:36)

Truly I love your commands more than gold,
even the finest gold.
(Psalm 119:127)

Come and show me your mercy,
as you do for all who love your name.
(Psalm 119:132)

Look upon me with love;
teach me your decrees.
(Psalm 119:135)

In your faithful love, O Lord, hear my cry;
let me be revived
by following your regulations.
(Psalm 119:149)

See how I love your commandments, Lord.
Give back my life
because of your unfailing love.
(Psalm 119:159)

I hate and abhor all falsehood,
but I love your instructions.
(Psalm 119:163)

Those who love your instructions
have great peace and do not stumble.
(Psalm 119:165)

I have obeyed your laws,
for I love them very much.
(Psalm 119:167)

O Israel, hope in the Lord;
for with the Lord there is unfailing love.
His redemption overflows.
(Psalm 130:7)

Give thanks to the Lord, for he is good!
His faithful love endures forever.
(Psalm 136:1)

I bow before your holy Temple
as I worship.
I praise your name
for your unfailing love and faithfulness;
for your promises are backed
by all the honor of your name.
(Psalm 138:2)

The Lord will work out his plans
for my life—
for your faithful love, O Lord, endures forever.
Don't abandon me,
for you made me.
(Psalm 138:8)

Let me hear
of your unfailing love each morning,
for I am trusting you.
Show me where to walk,
for I give myself to you.
(Psalm 143:8)

In your unfailing love,
silence all my enemies
and destroy all my foes,
for I am your servant.
(Psalm 143:12)

The Lord is merciful and compassionate,
slow to get angry
and filled with unfailing love.
(Psalm 145:8)

The Lord protects all those who love him,
but he destroys the wicked.
(Psalm 145:20)

The Lord opens the eyes of the blind.
The Lord lifts up
those who are weighed down.
The Lord loves the godly.
(Psalm 146:8)

The Lord's delight is in those who fear him,
those who put their hope
in his unfailing love.
(Psalm 147:11)

My child,
don't reject the Lord's discipline,
and don't be upset when he corrects you.
For the Lord corrects those he loves,
just as a father corrects
a child in whom he delights.
(Prov. 3:11-12)

Don't turn your back on wisdom,
for she will protect you.
Love her, and she will guard you.
(Prov. 4:6)

Drink water from your own well—
share your love only with your wife.
(Prov. 5:15)

Love wisdom like a sister;
make insight a beloved member of your family.
(Prov. 7:4)

"I(Wisdom) love all who love me.
Those who search will surely find me."
(Prov. 8:17)

So don't bother correcting mockers;
they will only hate you.
But correct the wise,
and they will love you.
(Prov. 9:8)

Hatred stirs up quarrels,
but love makes up for all offenses.
(Prov. 10:12)

Those who spare the rod of discipline
hate their children.
Those who love their children
care enough to discipline them.
(Prov. 13:24)

If you plan to do evil,
you will be lost;
if you plan to do good,
you will receive unfailing love and faithfulness.
(Prov. 14:22)

The Lord detests the way of the wicked,
but he loves those who pursue godliness.
(Prov. 15:9)

A bowl of vegetables with someone you love,
is better than steak with someone you hate.
(Prov. 15:17)

Unfailing love and faithfulness
make atonement for sin.
By fearing the Lord, people avoid evil.
(Prov. 16:6)

Love prospers when a fault is forgiven,
but dwelling on it separates close friends.
(Prov. 17:9)

To acquire wisdom is to love oneself;
people who cherish understanding will prosper.
(Prov. 19:8)

Whoever pursues righteousness
and unfailing love
will find life, righteousness and honor.
(Prov. 21:21)

An open rebuke
is better than hidden love.
(Prov. 27:5)

For everything there is a season,
a time for every activity under heaven.
A time to love and a time to hate.
A time for war and a time for peace.
(Eccles. 3:1,8)

Those who love money will never have enough.
How meaningless to think
that wealth brings true happiness!
(Eccles. 5:10)

Kiss me and kiss me again,
for your love is sweeter than wine.
(Song 1:2)

You are so handsome, my love,
pleasing beyond words!
(Song 1:16)

Your love delights me, my treasure, my bride.
Your love is better than wine,
Your perfume more fragrant than spices.
(Song 4:10)

I have entered my garden,
my treasure, my bride!
I gather myrrh with my spices
and eat honeycomb with my honey.
I drink wine with my milk.
Oh, lover and beloved, eat and drink!
Yes, drink deeply of your love!
(Song 5:1)

Oh, how beautiful you are!
How pleasing, my love, how full of delights!
(Song 7:6)

Come, my love, let us go out to the fields
and spend the night among the wildflowers.
Let us get up early
and go to the vineyards
to see if the grapevines have budded,
if the blossoms have opened,
and if the pomegranates have bloomed.
There I will give you my love.
(Song 7:11-12)

Promise me, O women of Jerusalem,
not to awaken love until the time is right.
(Song 8:4)

Place me like a seal over your heart,
like a seal on your arm.
For love is as strong as death,
its jealousy as enduring as the grave.
Love flashes like fire,
the brightest kind of flame.
Many waters cannot quench love,
nor can rivers drown it.
If a man tried to buy love with all his wealth,
his offer would be utterly scorned.
(Song 8:6-7)

# Chapter 16

# M

## MIRACLES

"If I were you I would go to God
and present my case to him.
He does great things too marvelous to understand.
He performs countless miracles."(Eliphaz)
(Job 5:8-9)

"His great works are too marvelous to understand.
He performs miracles without number."
(Job 9:10)

Now that I am old and gray,
do not abandon me, O God.
Let me proclaim your power
to this new generation,
your mighty miracles to all who come after me.
(Psalm 71:18)

Remember the wonders he has performed,
his miracles, and the rulings he has given.
(Psalm 105:5)

Who can list the glorious miracles of the Lord?
Who can ever praise him enough?
(Psalm 106:2)

Give thanks to him
who alone does mighty miracles.
His faithful love endures forever.
(Psalm 136:4)

## MONEY

"If you give up your lust for money
and throw your precious gold into the river,
the Almighty himself will be your treasure.
He will be your precious silver!" (Eliphaz)
(Job 22:24-25)

"Evil people may have piles of money
and may store away mounds of clothing.
But the righteous will wear that clothing
and the innocent will divide that money."
(Job 27:16-17)

"Have I put my trust in money
or felt secure because of my gold?
Have I gloated
about my wealth and all that I own?"
(Job 31:24-25)

Then all his brothers, sisters and former friends
came and feasted with him in his home.
And they consoled him and comforted him
because of all the trials the Lord had brought
against him. And each of them brought him
a gift of money and a gold ring."
(Job 42:11)

Those who lend money
without charging interest,
and who cannot be bribed
to lie about the innocent.
Such people will stand firm forever.
(Psalm 15:5)

Good comes to those
who lend money generously
and conduct their business fairly.
(Psalm 112:5)

Such is the fate of all who are greedy for money;
it robs them of life.
(Prov. 1:19)

Trust in your money and down you go!
But the godly flourish like leaves in spring.
(Prov. 11:28)

Those who love money will never have enough.
How meaningless to think
that wealth brings true happiness!
The more you have,
the more people come to help you spend it.
So what good is wealth—
except perhaps to watch it
slip through your fingers!
(Eccles. 5:10-11)

Hoarding riches harms the saver.
Money is put into risky investments
that turn sour,
and everything is lost.
In the end, there is nothing left
to pass on to one's children.
(Eccles. 5:14)

Wisdom is even better when you have money.
Both are a benefit as you go through life.
Wisdom and money
can get you almost anything,
but only wisdom can save your life.
(Eccles. 7:11-12)

A party gives laughter,
wine gives happiness,
and money gives everything!
(Eccles. 10:19)

## MOTIVE(S)

"Yet your real motive—your true intent—
was to watch me, and if I sinned,
you would not forgive my guilt."
(Job 10:13)

People may be pure in their own eyes,
but the Lord examines their motives.
(Prov. 16:2)

The Lord's light penetrates the human spirit,
exposing every hidden motive.
(Prov. 20:27)

The sacrifice of an evil person is detestable,
especially when it is offered with wrong motives.
(Prov. 21:27)

## MYSTERY (MYSTERIES)

"Can you solve the mysteries of God?
Can you discover everything about the Almighty?
Such knowledge is higher than the heavens."(Zophar)
(Job 11:7-8)

"He uncovers mysteries hidden in darkness;
he brings light to the deepest gloom."
(Job 12:22)

Just as you cannot understand
the path of the wind
or the mystery of a tiny baby
growing in its mother's womb,
so you cannot understand the activity of God,
who does all things.
(Eccles. 11:5)

# Chapter 17

## N

### NAKED

He said,
"I came naked from my mother's womb,
and I will be naked when I leave.
The Lord gave me what I had,
and the Lord has taken it away.
Praise the name of the Lord!"
(Job 1:21)

"The underworld is naked in God's presence.
The place of destruction is uncovered.
(Job 26:6)

We all come to the end of our lives as naked
and empty-handed as on the day we were born.
We can't take our riches with us.
(Eccles. 5:15)

## NATION

What joy for the nation whose God is the Lord,
whose people he has chosen as his inheritance.
(Psalm 33:12)

Without wise leadership, a nation falls;
there is safety in having many advisers.
(Prov. 11:14)

Godliness makes a nation great,
but sin is a disgrace to any people.
(Prov. 14:34)

When there is moral rot within a nation,
its government topples easily.
But wise and knowledgeable leaders bring stability.
(Prov. 28:2)

A just king gives stability to his nation,
but one who demands bribes destroys it.
(Prov. 29:4)

## NEIGHBOR

Do not withhold good
from those who deserve it
when it is in your power to help them.
If you can help your neighbor now, don't say,
"Come back tomorrow, and then I'll help you."
Don't plot harm against your neighbor,
for those who live nearby trust you.
(Prov. 3:27-29)

It is foolish to belittle one's neighbor;
a sensible person keeps quiet.
(Prov. 11:12)

Don't visit your neighbors too often,
or you will wear out your welcome.
(Prov. 25:17)

When disaster strikes,
you won't have to ask your brother for assistance.
It is better to go to a neighbor
than to a brother who lives far away.
(Prov. 27:10)

## NEEDY

"The poor are pushed off the path;
the needy must hide together for safety."
(Job 24:4)

"The murderer rises in the early dawn
to kill the poor and needy;
at night he is a thief."
(Job 24:14)

"They(wicked) cheat the woman
who has no son to help her.
They refuse to help the needy widow."
(Job 24:21)

"Surely no one would turn against the needy
when they cry for help in their trouble.
Did I not weep for those in trouble?
Was I not deeply grieved for the needy?"
(Job 30: 24-25)

"Whenever I saw the homeless without clothes
and the needy with nothing to wear,
did they not praise me
for providing wool clothing to keep them warm?"
(Job 31:19)

"They(wicked) cause the poor to cry out,
catching God's attention.
He hears the cries of the needy."(Elihu)
(Job 34:28)

But the needy will not be ignored forever;
the hopes of the poor will not always be crushed.
(Psalm 9:18)

For he has not ignored or belittled
the suffering of the needy.
He has not turned his back on them,
but has listened to their cries for help.
(Psalm 22:24)

As for me, since I am poor and needy,
let the Lord keep me in his thoughts.
You are my helper and my savior.
O my God, do not delay.
(Psalm 40:17)

For the Lord hears the cries of the needy;
he does not despise his imprisoned people.
(Psalm 69:33)

He(God) feels pity for the weak and the needy,
and he will rescue them.
(Psalm 72:13)

Don't let the downtrodden be humiliated again.
Instead, let the poor and needy praise your name.
(Psalm 74:21)

For I am poor and needy,
and my heart is full of pain.
(Psalm 109:22)

For he(God) stands beside the needy,
ready to save them
from those who condemn them.
(Psalm 109:31)

He(God) lifts the poor from the dust
and the needy from the garbage dump.
(Psalm 113:7)

Don't rob the poor just because you can,
or exploit the needy in court.
(Prov. 22:22)

She(virtuous wife) extends
a helping hand to the poor
and opens her arms to the needy.
(Prov. 31:20)

## NOTHING CERTAIN

Enjoy prosperity while you can;
but when hard times strike,
realize that both come from God.
Remember that nothing is certain in this life.
(Eccles. 7:14)

## NOTHING NEW

History merely repeats itself.
It has all been done before.
Nothing under the sun is truly new.
Sometimes people say,
"Here is something new!"
But actually, it is old;
nothing is ever truly new.
We don't remember what happened in the past,
and in future generations,
no one will remember what we are doing now.
(Eccles. 1:9-11)

And I know that whatever God does is final.
Nothing can be added to it or taken from it.
God's purpose is that people should fear him.
What is happening now has happened before,
and what will happen in the future
has happened before,
because God makes the same things happen
over and over again.
(Eccles. 3:14-15)

# Chapter 18

# O

## OPPRESSED(OPPRESSION)

"What do you(God) gain by oppressing me?
Why do you reject me,
the work of your own hands,
while smiling on the schemes of the wicked?"
(Job 10:3)

"For they(godless) oppressed the poor
and left them destitute.
They foreclosed on their homes."(Zophar)
(Job 20:19)

"I broke the jaws of godless oppressors
and plucked their victims from their teeth."
(Job 29:17)

The Lord is a shelter for the oppressed,
a refuge in times of trouble.
(Psalm 9:9)

You(God) will bring justice
to the orphans and the oppressed,
so mere people can no longer terrify them.
(Psalm 10:18)

Therefore, Lord,
we know you will protect the oppressed,
preserving them forever
from this lying generation.
(Psalm 12:7)

The wicked frustrate the plans of the oppressed,
but the Lord will protect his people.
(Psalm 14:6)

The wicked draw their swords
and string their bows
to kill the poor and the oppressed,
to slaughter those who do right.
(Psalm 37:14)

"O God, my rock," I cry,
"why have you forgotten me?
Why must I wander around in grief,
oppressed by my enemies?"
(Psalm 42:9)

Why do you(God) look the other way?
Why do you ignore
our suffering and oppression?
(Psalm 44:24)

My God,
rescue me from the power of the wicked,
from the clutches of cruel oppressors.
(Psalm 71:4)

He(God) will rescue the poor
when they cry to him;
he will help the oppressed,
who have no one to defend them.
(Psalm 72:12)

He(God) will redeem them
from oppression and violence,
for their lives are precious to him.
(Psalm 72:14)

You stand up to judge
those who do evil, O God,
and to rescue the oppressed of the earth.
(Psalm 76:9)

Give justice to the poor and the orphan;
uphold the rights
of the oppressed and the destitute.
(Psalm 82:3)

But these oppressors know nothing;
they are ignorant!
They wander about in darkness,
while the whole world is shaken to the core.
(Psalm 82:5)

Please guarantee a blessing for me.
Don't let the arrogant oppress me!
(Psalm 119:122)

Ransom me from the oppression of evil people;
then I can obey your commandments.
(Psalm 119:134)

He(God) gives justice to the oppressed
and food to the hungry.
(Psalm 146:7)

A person who gets ahead
by oppressing the poor
or by showering gifts on the rich,
will end in poverty.
(Prov. 22:16)

A poor person who oppresses the poor
is like a pounding rain that destroys the crops.
(Prov. 28:3)

A ruler with no understanding
will oppress his people,
but one who hates corruption
will have a long life.
(Prov. 28:16)

The poor and the oppressor have this in common—
the Lord gives sight to the eyes of both.
(Prov. 29:13)

It is not for kings, O Lemuel,
to guzzle wine.
Rulers should not crave alcohol.
For if they drink,
they may forget the law
and not give justice to the oppressed.
(Prov. 31:4-5)

Again, I observed all the oppression
that takes place under the sun.
I saw the tears of the oppressed,
with no one to comfort them.
The oppressors have great power
and their victims are helpless.
So I concluded
that the dead are better off than the living.
But most fortunate of all
are those who are not yet born.
For they have not seen
all the evil that is done under the sun.
(Eccles. 4:1-3)

Don't be surprised if you see a poor person
being oppressed by the powerful
and if justice is being miscarried throughout the land.
For every official is under orders from higher up,
and matters of justice get lost in red tape and bureau-
cracy.
(Eccles. 5:8)

# Chapter 19

# P

## PARTIALITY

Showing partiality is never good,
yet some will do wrong for a mere piece of bread.
(Prov. 28:21)

## PATIENCE (PATIENT)

Better to be patient than powerful;
better to have self-contol than to conquer a city.
(Prov. 16:32)

Finishing is better than starting.
Patience is better than pride.
(Eccles. 7:8)

## POWER

"And if I hold my head high,
you(God) hunt me like a lion
and display your awesome power against me."
(Job 10:16)

"People who are at ease mock those in trouble.
They give a push to people who are stumbling.
But robbers are left in peace,
and those who provoke God live in safety—
though God keeps them in his power."
(Job 12:5-6)

"But true wisdom and power are found in God;
counsel and understanding are his."
( Job 12:13)

"Yes, strength and wisdom are his;
deceivers and deceived are both in his power."
(Job 12:16)

"He leads priests away, stripped of status;
he overthrows those with long years in power."
(Job 12:19)

"God in his power, drags away the rich.
They may rise high,
but they have no assurance of life."
(Job 24:22)

"By his power the sea grew calm.
By his skill he crushed the great sea monster.
His Spirit made the heavens beautiful,
and his power pierced the gliding serpent.
These are just the beginning of all that he does,
merely a whisper of his power.
Who, then, can comprehend
the thunder of his power."
(Job 26:12-14)

"I will teach you about God' power.
I will not conceal anything concerning the Almighty."
(Job 27:11)

"I cry to you, O God, but you don't answer.
I stand before you, but you don't even look.
You have become cruel toward me.
You use your power to persecute me."
(Job 30:20-21)

"People cry out when they are oppressed.
They groan beneath the power of the Almighty."(Elihu)
(Job 35:9)

"God is mighty, but he does not despise anyone!
He is mighty
in both power and understanding."(Elihu)
(Job 36:5)

"God's voice is glorious in the thunder.
We can't even imagine the greatness of his power.
He directs the snow to fall on the earth
and tells the rain to pour down.
Then everyone stops working
so they can watch his power."(Elihu)
(Job 37:5-7)

"We cannot imagine the power of the Almighty;
but even though he is just and righteous,
he does not destroy us.
No wonder people everywhere fear him.
All who are wise show him reverence."(Elihu)
(Job 37:23-24)

Show me your unfailing love in wonderful ways.
By your mighty power you rescue those
who seek refuge from their enemies.
(Psalm 17:7)

By the power of your hand, O Lord,
destroy those who look to this world
for their reward.
But satisfy the hunger of your treasured ones.
May their children have plenty,
leaving an inheritance for their descendants.
(Psalm 17:14)

The Lord is my rock, my fortress, and my savior;
my God is my rock in whom I find protection.
He is my shield, the power that saves me,
and my place of safety.
(Psalm 18:2)

Rise up, O Lord, in all your power.
With music and singing
we celebrate your mighty acts.
(Psalm 21:13)

For royal power belongs to the Lord.
He rules all nations.
(Psalm 22:28)

I have not kept the good news of your justice
hidden in my heart;
I have talked about your faithfulness
and saving power.
I have told everyone in the great assembly
of your unfailing love and faithfulness.
(Psalm 40:10)

You drove out the pagan nations by your power
and gave all the land to our ancestors.
You crushed their enemies
and set our ancestors free.
(Psalm 44:2)

Only by your power
can we push back our enemies;
only in your name
can we trample our foes.
(Psalm 44:5)

Come with great power, O God, and rescue me!
Defend me with your might.
(Psalm 54:1)

Don't kill them,
for my people soon forget such lessons;
stagger them with your power,
and bring them to their knees,
O Lord, our shield.
(Psalm 59:11)

Now rescue your beloved people.
Answer and save us by your power.
(Psalm 60:5)

I have seen you in your sanctuary
and gazed upon your power and glory.
(Psalm 63:2)

You formed the mountains by your power
and armed yourself with mighty strength.
(Psalm 65:6)

Say to God,
"How awesome are your deeds!
Your enemies cringe before your mighty power."
(Psalm 66:3)

For by his great power he rules forever.
He watches every movement of the nations;
let no rebel rise in defiance.
(Psalm 66:7)

May your ways be known throughout the earth,
your saving power among people everywhere.
(Psalm 67:2)

Summon your might, O God.
Display your power, O God,
as you have in the past.
(Psalm 68:28)

Tell everyone about God's power.
His majesty shines down on Israel;
his strength is mighty in the heavens.
God is awesome in his sanctuary.
The God of Israel
gives power and strength to his people.
Praise be to God!
(Psalm 68:34-35)

I am suffering and in pain.
Rescue me, O God, by your saving power.
(Psalm 69:29)

My God,
rescue me from the power of the wicked,
from the clutches of cruel oppressors.
(Psalm 71:4)

I will tell everyone about your righteousness.
All day long I will proclaim your saving power,
though I am not skilled in words.
(Psalm 71:15)

Now that I am old and gray,
do not abandon me, O God.
Let me proclaim your power
to this new generation,
your mighty miracles
to all who come after me.
(Psalm 71:18)

For God says,
"I will break the strength of the wicked,
but I will increase the power of the godly."
(Psalm 75:10)

You are the God of great wonders!
You demonstrate your awesome power
among the nations.
(Psalm 77:14)

We will not hide these truths from our children;
we will tell the next generation
about the glorious deeds of the Lord,
about his power and his mighty wonders.
(Psalm 78:4)

No one can live forever;
all will die.
No one can escape the power of the grave.
(Psalm 89:48)

Who can comprehend the power of your anger?
Your wrath is as awesome
as the fear you deserve.
(Psalm 90:11)

You who love the Lord, hate evil!
He protects the lives of his godly people,
and rescues them from the power of the wicked.
(Psalm 97:10)

Sing a new song to the Lord,
for he has done wonderful deeds.
His right hand has won a mighty victory;
his holy arm has shown his saving power!
(Psalm 98:1)

Our ancestors in Egypt
were not impressed
by the Lord's miraculous deeds.
They soon forgot
his many acts of kindness to them.
Instead, they rebelled against him at the Red Sea.
Even so, he saved them—
to defend the honor of his name
and to demonstrate his mighty power.
(Psalm 106:7-8)

Some went off to sea in ships,
plying the trade routes of the world.
They, too, observed the Lord's power in action,
his impressive works on the deepest seas.
(Psalm 107:23-24)

Be exalted, O God,
above the highest heavens.
May your glory shine over all the earth.
Now rescue your beloved people.
Answer and save us by your power.
(Psalm 108:5-6)

He gives food to those who fear him;
he always remembers his covenant.
He has shown his great power to his people
by giving them the lands of other nations.
(Psalm 111:5-6)

Reach down from heaven and rescue me;
rescue me from deep waters,
from the power of my enemies.
(Psalm 144:7)

Let each generation tell its children
of your mighty acts;
let them proclaim your power.
(Psalm 145:4)

All of your works will thank you, Lord,
and your faithful followers will praise you.
They will speak of the glory of your Kingdom;
they will give examples of your power.
(Psalm 145:10-11)

How great is our Lord!
His power is absolute!
His understanding is beyond comprehension!
(Psalm 147:5)

Do not withhold good
from those who deserve it
when it's in your power to help them.
(Prov. 3:27)

When the godly are in authority,
the people rejoice.
When the wicked are in power, they groan.
(Prov.29:2)

None of us can hold back
our spirit from departing.
None of us has the power
to prevent the day of our death.
There is no escaping that obligation,
that dark battle.
(Eccles.8:8)

## PRAY (PRAYER)

"But if you pray to God
and seek the favor of the Almighty,
and if you are pure and live with integrity,
he will surely rise up
and restore your happy home.
And though you started with little,
you will end with much."(Bildad)
(Job 8:5-7)

"If only you would prepare your heart
and lift up your hands to him in prayer!
Get rid of your sins,
and leave all iniquity behind you.
Then your face will brighten with innocence.
You will be strong and free of fear."(Zophar)
(Job 11:13-15)

"My eyes are red with weeping;
dark shadows circle my eyes.
Yet I have done no wrong
and my prayer is pure."
(Job 16:16-17)

"They(wicked) spend their days in prosperity,
then go down to the grave in peace.
And yet they say to God,
"Go away.
We want no part of you and your ways.
Who is the Almighty
and why should we obey him?
What good will it do us to pray?
(Job 21:13-15)

"Then you will take delight in the Almighty
and look up to God.
You will pray to him,
and he will hear you,
and you will fulfill your vows to him."(Eliphaz)
(Job 22:26-27)

"When he prays to God, he will be accepted.
And God will receive him with joy
and restore him to good standing."(Elihu)
(Job 33:26)

After the Lord had finished speaking to Job,
he said to Eliphaz the Temanite: "I am angry
with you and your two friends, for you have
not spoken accurately about me, as my servant
Job has. So take seven bulls and seven rams
and go to my servant Job and offer a burnt
offering for yourselves. My servant Job will
pray for you, and I will accept his prayer on
your behalf. I will not treat you as you deserve,
for you have not spoken accurately about me,
as my servant Job has."
So Eliphaz the Temanite, Bildad the Shuhite,
and Zophar the Naamathite did as the Lord
commanded them, and the Lord accepted
Job's prayer.

(Job 42:7-9)

Answer me when I call to you, O God,
who declares me innocent.
Free me from my troubles.
Have mercy on me and hear my prayer.

(Psalm 4:1)

O Lord, hear me as I pray;
pay attention to my groaning.
Listen to my cry for help,
my King and my God,
for I pray to no one but you.

(Psalm 5:1-2)

The Lord has heard my plea;
the Lord will answer my prayer.
May all my enemies
be disgraced and terrified.
May they suddenly turn back in shame.
(Psalm 6:9-10)

Will those who do evil never learn?
They eat up my people like bread
and wouldn't think of praying to the Lord.
(Psalm 14:4)

O Lord, hear my plea for justice.
Listen to my cry for help.
Pay attention to my prayer,
for it comes from honest lips.
(Psalm 17:1)

I am praying to you
because I know you will answer, O God.
Bend down and listen as I pray.
(Psalm 17:6)

But in my distress I cried out to the Lord,
yes, I prayed to my God for help.
He heard me from his sanctuary;
my cry to him reached his ears.
(Psalm 18:6)

May he grant your heart's desires
and make all your plans succeed.
May we shout for joy
when we hear of your victory
and raise a victory banner
in the name of our God.
May the Lord answer all your prayers.
(Psalm 20:4-5)

Hear me as I pray, O Lord.
Be merciful and answer me!
(Psalm 27:7)

I pray to you, O Lord, my rock.
Do not turn a deaf ear to me.
For if you are silent,
I might as well give up and die.
Listen to my prayer for mercy
as I cry out to you for help,
as I lift my hands toward your holy sanctuary.
(Psalm 28:1-2)

Therefore, let all the godly pray to you
while there is still time,
that they may not drown
in the floodwaters of judgment.
(Psalm 32:6)

I prayed to the Lord
and he answered me.
He freed me from all my fears.
(Psalm 34:4)

In my desperation I prayed
and the Lord listened;
he saved me from all my troubles.
(Psalm 34:6)

Malicious witnesses testify against me.
They accuse me of crimes
I know nothing about.
They repay me evil for good.
I am sick with despair.
Yet when they were ill, I grieved for them.
I denied myself by fasting for them,
but my prayers returned unanswered.
(Psalm 35:11-13)

Hear my prayer, O Lord!
Listen to my cries for help!
Don't ignore my tears.
For I am your guest—a traveler passing through,
as my ancestors were before me.
(Psalm 39:12)

I will praise you as long I live,
lifting up my hands to you in prayer.
(Psalm 63:4)

What mighty praise, O God,
belongs to you in Zion.
We will fulfill our vows to you,
for you answer our prayers.
All of us must come to you.
(Psalm 65:1-2)

You faithfully answer our prayers
with awesome deeds, O God, our Savior.
You are the hope of everyone on earth,
even those who sail on distant seas.
(Psalm 65:5)

But God did listen!
He paid attention to my prayer.
Praise God,
who did not ignore my prayer
or withdraw his unfailing love from me.
(Psalm 66:19-20)

But I keep praying to you, Lord,
hoping this time you will show me favor.
In your unfailing love, O God,
answer my prayer with your sure salvation.
(Psalm 69:13)

Answer my prayers, O Lord,
for your unfailing love is wonderful.
Take care of me,
for your mercy is so plentiful.
(Psalm 69:16)

When I was in deep trouble,
I searched for the Lord.
All night long I prayed,
with hands lifted toward heaven,
but my soul was not comforted.
(Psalm 77:2)

You don't let me sleep.
I am too distressed even to pray!
(Psalm 77:4)

O Lord God of Heaven's Armies,
how long will you be angry with our prayers?
(Psalm 80:4)

O Lord God of Heaven's Armies,
hear my prayer.
Listen, O God of Jacob.
(Psalm 84:8)

Bend down, O Lord, and hear my prayer;
answer me, for I need your help.
(Psalm 86:1)

Listen closely to my prayer, O Lord;
hear my urgent cry.
(Psalm 86:6)

O Lord, God of my salvation,
I cry out to you by day.
I come to you at night.
Now hear my prayer;
listen to my cry.
(Psalm 88:1-2)

Lord, hear my prayer!
Listen to my plea!
Don't turn away from me
in my time of distress.
Bend down to listen,
and answer me quickly when I call to you.
(Psalm 102:1-2)

For the Lord will rebuild Jerusalem
He will appear in his glory.
He will listen to the prayers of the destitute.
He will not reject their pleas.
(Psalm 102:16-17)

They(wicked) surround me with hateful words
and fight against me for no reason.
I love them,
but they try to destroy me with accusations
even as I am praying for them!
They repay evil for good,
and hatred for my love.
They say, "Get an evil person to turn against him.
Send an accuser to bring him to trial.
When his case comes up for judgment,
let him be pronounced guilty.
Count his prayers as sins."
(Psalm 109:3-7)

I love the Lord because he hears my voice
and my prayer for mercy.
Because he bends down to listen,
I will pray as long as I have breath!
(Psalm 116:1-2)

In my distress I prayed to the Lord,
and the Lord answered me and set me free.
(Psalm 118:5)

I thank you for answering my prayer
and giving me victory!
(Psalm 118:21)

I pray with all my heart;
answer me, Lord!
I will obey your decrees.
(Psalm 119:145)

O Lord, listen to my cry;
give me the discerning mind you promised.
Listen to my prayer;
rescue me as you promised.
(Psalm 119:169-170)

I took my troubles to the Lord;
I cried out to him,
and he answered my prayer.
(Psalm 120:1)

From the depths of despair, O Lord,
I call for your help.
Hear my cry, O Lord.
Pay attention to my prayer.
(Psalm 130:2)

Oh, praise the Lord,
all you servants of the Lord,
you who serve at night
in the house of the Lord.
Lift up holy hands in prayer,
and praise the Lord.
(Psalm 134:1-2)

As soon as I pray,
you answer me;
you encourage me by giving me strength.
(Psalm 138:3)

O Lord, I am calling to you.
Please hurry!
Listen when I cry to you for help!
Accept my prayer
as incense offered to you,
and my upraised hands as an evening offering.
(Psalm 141:1-2)

Let the godly strike me!
It will be a kindness!
If they correct me, it is soothing medicine.
Don't let me refuse it.
But I pray constantly
against the wicked and their deeds.
(Psalm 141:5)

I look for someone to come and help me,
but no one gives me a passing thought!
No one will help me;
no one cares a bit what happens to me.
Then I pray to you, O Lord.
I say, "You are my place of refuge.
You are all I really want in life."
(Psalm 142:4-5)

Hear my prayer, O Lord;
listen to my plea!
Answer me because you are faithful and righteous
(Psalm 143:1)

I remember the days of old.
I ponder all your great works
and think about what you have done.
I lift my hands to you in prayer.
I thirst for you
as parched land thirsts for rain.
(Psalm 143:5-6)

## PRIDE (PROUD)

"Again and again he smashes against me,
charging at me like a warrior.
I wear burlap to show my grief.
My pride lies in the dust."
(Job 16:14-15)

"Though the pride of the godless
reaches to the heavens
and their heads touch the clouds,
yet they will vanish forever,
thrown away like their own dung.
Those who know them will ask,
'Where are they?'"(Zophar)
(Job 20:6-7)

"And when they(proud) cry out,
God does not answer because of their pride.
But it is wrong to say God doesn't listen,
to say the Almighty isn't concerned."(Elihu)
(Job 35:12-13)

"If they(innocent) are bound in chains
and caught up in a web of trouble,
he shows them the reason
He shows them their sins of pride.
He gets their attention
and commands that they turn from evil."(Elihu)
(Job 36:8-10)

O God, you take no pleasure in wickedness;
you cannot tolerate the sins of the wicked.
Therefore, the proud may not stand
in your presence,
for you hate all who do evil.
(Psalm 5:4-5)

You rescue the humble,
but you humiliate the proud.
(Psalm 18:27)

Don't let me be disgraced, O Lord.
for I call out to you for help.
Let the wicked be disgraced;
Let them be silent in the grave.
Silence their lying lips—
those proud and arrogant lips
that accuse the godly.
(Psalm 31:17-18)

Oh, the joys of those who trust the Lord,
who have no confidence in the proud
or in those who worship idols!
(Psalm 40:4)

Because of the sinful things they say,
because of the evil that is on their lips,
let them be captured by their pride,
their curses and their lies.
(Psalm 59:12)

But as for me, I almost lost my footing.
My feet were slipping,
and I was almost gone.
For I envied the proud
when I saw them prosper
despite their wickedness.
(Psalm 73:2-3)

They(proud) wear pride like a jeweled necklace
and clothe themselves with cruelty.
These fat cats have everything
their hearts could ever wish for!
They scoff and speak only evil;
in their pride they seek to crush others.
(Psalm 73:6-8)

I will reject perverse ideas
and stay away from every evil.
I will not tolerate people
who slander their neighbors.
I will not endure conceit and pride.
(Psalm 101:4-5)

Have mercy on us, Lord, have mercy,
for we have had our fill of contempt.
We have had more than our fill
of the scoffing of the proud
and the contempt of the arrogant.
(Psalm 123:3-4)

Lord, my heart is not proud;
my eyes are not haughty.
I do not concern myself with matters
too great or awesome for me to grasp.
(Psalm 131:1)

The proud have set a trap to catch me;
they have stretched out a net;
they have placed traps all along the way.
(Psalm 140:5)

Lord, do not let evil people have their way.
Do not let their evil schemes succeed,
or they will become proud.
(Psalm 140:8)

All who fear the Lord will hate evil.
Therefore, I hate pride and arrogance,
corruption and perverse speech.
(Prov. 8:13)

Pride leads to disgrace,
but with humility comes wisdom.
(Prov. 11:2)

Pride leads to conflict;
those who take advice are wise.
(Prov. 13:10)

Pride goes before destruction,
and haughtiness before a fall.
Beter to live humbly with the poor
than to share plunder with the proud.
(Prov. 16:18-19)

Grandchildren are the crowning glory of the aged;
parents are the pride of their children.
(Prov. 17:6)

Haughty eyes, a proud heart
and evil actions are all sin.
(Prov. 21:4)

Pride ends in humiliation,
while humility brings honor.
(Prov. 29:23)

If you have been a fool
by being proud or plotting evil,
cover your mouth with shame.
(Prov.30:32)

## PROFIT

Plant your seed in the morning
and keep busy all afternoon,
for you don't know if profit will come
from one activity or another—or both.
(Eccles. 11:6)

PROMISE(S)

The Lord's promises are pure,
like silver refined in a furnace,
purified seven times over.
Therefore, Lord,
we know you will protect the oppressed,
preserving them forever
from this lying generation.
(Psalm 12:6-7)

Those who refuse to gossip or harm their neighbors,
or speak evil of their friends.
Those who despise flagrant sinners,
and honor the faithful followers of the Lord,
and keep their promises even when it hurts.
Those who lend money without charging interest,
and who cannot be bribed
to lie about the innocent.
Such people will stand firm forever.
(Psalm 12:3-5)

God's way is perfect.
All the Lord's promises prove true.
He is a shield
for all who look to him for protection.
(Psalm 18:30)

Reassure me of your promise,
made to those who fear you.
(Psalm 119:38)

Remember your promise to me;
it is my only hope.
Your promise revives me;
it comforts me in all my troubles.
(Psalm 119:49-50)

Lord, you are mine!
I promise to obey your words!
(Psalm 119:57)

Your promises have been thoroughly tested;
that is why I love them so much.
(Psalm 119:140)

The Lord always keeps his promises;
he is gracious in all he does.
(Psalm 145:13)

He made heaven and earth,
the sea and everything I them.
He keeps every promise forever.
(Psalm 146:6)

Don't trap yourself
by making a rash promise to God
and only later counting the cost.
(Prov. 20:25)

When you make a promise to God,
don't delay in following through,
for God takes no pleasure in fools.
Keep all the promises you make to him.
It is better to say nothing
than to make a promise and not keep it.
(Eccles. 5:4-5)

# Chapter 20

# Q

## QUARREL

Starting a quarrel is like opening a floodgate,
so stop before a dispute breaks out.
(Prov. 17:14)

Fire goes out without wood,
and quarrels disappear when gossip stops.
A quarrelsome person starts fights
as easily as hot embers light charcoal
or fire lights wood.
(Prov. 26:20-21)

# Chapter 21

# R

## REDEEMER

"But as for me, I know that my Redeemer lives
and he will stand upon the earth at last.
And after my body has decayed,
yet in my body I will see God!
I will see him for myself.
Yes, I will see him with my own eyes.
I am overwhelmed at the thought!"
(Job 19:25-27)

May the words of my mouth
and the meditation of my heart
be pleasing to you,
O Lord, my rock and my redeemer.
(Psalm 19:14)

## REPUTATION

Choose a good reputation over great riches;
being held in high esteem
is better than silver or gold.
(Prov. 22:1)

A good reputation
is more valuable than costly perfume.
And the day you die
is better than the day you were born.
(Eccles. 7:1)

## RESENTMENT

A stone is heavy and sand is weighty,
but the resentment caused by a fool is even heavier.
(Prov. 27:3)

## REWARD(S)

"The heavens will reveal their guilt,
and the earth will testify against them.
A flood will sweep away their house.
God's anger will descend on them in torrents.
This is the reward that God gives to the wicked.
It is the inheritance decreed by God."(Zophar)
(Job 20:27-29)

By the power of your hand, O Lord,
destroy those who look to this world for their reward.
But satisfy the hunger of your treasured ones.
May their children have plenty,
leaving an inheritance for their descendants.
(Psalm 17:14)

The Lord rewarded me for doing right;
he restored me because of my innocence.
(Psalm 18:20)

The laws of the Lord are true;
each one is fair.
They are more desirable than gold,
even the finest gold.
They are sweeter than honey,
even honey dripping from the comb.
They are a warning to your servant,
a great reward for those who obey them.
(Psalm 19:9-11)

The Lord says,
"I will rescue those who love me.
I will protect those who trust in my name.
When they call on me, I will answer;
I will be with them in trouble.
I will rescue and honor them.
I will reward them with a long life
and give them my salvation."
(Psalm 91:14-16)

Your kindness will reward you,
but your cruelty will destroy you.
(Prov. 11:17)

Evil people get rich for the moment,
but the reward of the godly will last.
(Prov. 11:18)

The godly can look forward to a reward,
while the wicked can expect only judgment.
(Prov. 11:23)

Wise words bring many benefits,
and hard work brings rewards.
(Prov. 12:14)

Backsliders get what they deserve;
good people receive their reward.
(Prov. 14:14)

Don't envy sinners,
but always continue to fear the Lord.
You will be rewarded for this;
your hope will not be disappointed.
(Prov. 23:17-18)

If your enemies are hungry,
give them food to eat.
If they are thirsty
give them water to drink.
You will heap burning coals of shame on their heads,
and the Lord will reward you.
(Prov. 25:21-22)

As workers who tend a fig tree
are allowed to eat the fruit,
so workers who protect
their employer's interests will be rewarded.
(Prov. 27:18)

So I became greater
than all who had lived in Jerusalem before me,
and my wisdom never failed me.
Anything I wanted, I would take.
I denied myself no pleasure.
I even found great pleasure in hard work,
a reward for all my labor.
But as I looked at everything
I had worked so hard to accomplish,
it was all meaningless—
like chasing the wind.
There was nothing really worthwhile anywhere.
(Eccles. 2:9-11)

## RIGHT

"Look at me!
Would I lie to your face?
Stop assuming my guilt,
for I have done no wrong.
Do you think I am lying?
Don't I know the difference
between right and wrong?"
(Job 6:28-30)

"How long will you go on like this?
You sound like a blustering wind.
Does God twist justice?
Does the Almighty twist what is right?"(Bildad)
(Job 8:2-3)

"So who am I that I should try to answer God
or even reason with him?
Even if I were right,
I would have no defense.
I could only plead for mercy."
(Job 9:14-15)

"I vow by the living God,
who has taken away my rights,
by the Almighty who has embittered my soul—
as long as I live,
while I have breath from God,
my lips will speak no evil,
and my tongue will speak no lies.
I will never concede that you are right;
I will defend my integrity until I die."
(Job 27:2-5)

"So let us discern for ourselves what is right;
let us learn together what is good.
For Job also said, I am innocent,
but God has taken away my rights.'"(Elihu)
(Job 34: 4-5)

"Brace yourself like a man,
because I have some questions for you,
and you must answer them.
Will you discredit my justice
and condemn me just to prove you are right?
Are you as strong as God?
Can you thunder with a voice like his?"
(God's questions to Job)
(Job 40:7-9)

Lead me in the right path, O Lord
or my enemies will conquer me.
make your way plain for me to follow.
(Psalm 5:8)

God is my shield,
saving those whose hearts are true and right.
(Psalm 7:10)

The wicked are stringing their bows
and fitting their arrows on the bowstrings.
They shoot from the shadows
at those whose hearts are right.
(Psalm 11:2)

Declare me innocent,
for you see those who do right.
(Psalm 17:2)

The Lord rewarded me for doing right;
he restored me because of my innocence.
(Psalm 18:20)

The commandments of the Lord are right,
bringing joy to the heart.
The commands of the Lord are clear,
giving insight for living.
(Psalm 19:8)

He renews my strength,
He guides me along right paths,
bringing honor to his name.
(Psalm 23:3)

They will receive the Lord's blessing
and have a right relationship
with God their savior.
Such people may seek you
and worship in your presence, O God of Jacob.
(Psalm 24:5-6)

Show me the right path, O Lord;
point out the road for me to follow.
(Psalm 25:4)

The Lord is good
and does what is right;
he shows the proper path
to those who go astray.
He leads the humble in doing right,
teaching them his way.
(Psalm 25:8-9)

Teach me how to live, O Lord.
Lead me along the right path,
for my enemies are waiting for me.
(Psalm 27:11)

The eyes of the Lord
watch over those who do right;
his ears are open to their cries for help.
(Psalm 34:15)

Against you, and you alone, have I sinned;
I have done what is evil in your sight.
You will be proved right in what you say,
and your judgment against me is just.
(Psalm 51:4)

The godly will rejoice in the Lord
and find shelter in him.
And those who do what is right will praise him.
(Psalm 64:10)

Save me and rescue me,
for you do what is right.
Turn your ear to listen to me,
and set me free.
(Psalm 71:2)

For the Lord God is our sun and shield.
He gives us grace and glory.
The Lord will withhold no good thing
from those who do what is right.
(Psalm 84:11)

Light shines on the godly,
and joy on those whose hearts are right.
(Psalm 97:11)

There is joy for those who deal justly with others
and always do what is right.
(Psalm 106:3)

Don't leave me to the mercy of my enemies,
for I have done what is just and right.
(Psalm 119:121)

Each of your commandments is right.
That is why I hate every false way.
(Psalm 119:128)

Your laws are always right;
help me to understand them so I may live.
(Psalm 119:144)

Let my tongue sing about your word,
for all of your commands are right.
(Psalm 119:172)

He guards the paths of the just
and protects those who are faithful to him,.
Then you will understand
what is right, just and fair,
and you will find the right way to go.
(Prov. 2:8-9)

Wisdom will save you from evil people,
from those whose words are twisted.
These men turn from the right way
to walk down dark paths.
(Prov. 2:12-13)

Listen to me!
For I have important things to tell you.
Every thing I say is right,
for I speak the truth
and detest every kind of deception.
(Prov. 8:6-7)

Tainted wealth has no lasting value,
but right living can save your life.
(Prov. 10:2)

Riches won't help on the day of judgment,
but right living can save you from death.
(Prov. 11:4)

Fools think their own way is right,
but the wise listen to others.
(Prov. 12:15)

Those who follow the right path fear the Lord;
those who take the wrong path despise him.
(Prov. 14:2)

There is a path before each person that seems right,
but it ends in death.
(Prov. 14:12)

Whoever abandons the right path
will be severely disciplined;
whoever hates correction will die.
(Prov. 15:10)

Foolishness brings joy to those with no sense;
a sensible person stays on the right path.
(Prov. 15:21)

Everyone enjoys a fitting reply;
it is wonderful
to say the right thing at the right time!
(Prov. 15:23)

We can make our own plans,
but the Lord gives the right answer.
(Prov. 16:1)

It is not right to acquit the guilty
or deny justice to the innocent.
(Prov. 18:5)

Wise words satisfy like a good meal;
the right words bring satisfaction.
(Prov. 18:20)

People may be right in their own eyes,
but the Lord examines their heart.
(Prov. 21:2)

The Lord is more pleased
when we do what is right and just
than when we offer him sacrifices.
(Prov. 21:3)

Direct your children onto the right path,
and when they are older,
they will not leave it.
(Prov. 22:6)

Everything in me will celebrate
when you speak what is right.
(Prov. 23:16)

My child, listen and be wise;
keep your heart on the right course.
(Prov. 23:19)

What is wrong cannot be made right.
What is missing cannot be recovered.
(Eccles.1:15)

Those who are wise
will find a time and a way to do what is right,
for there is a time and a way for everything,
even when a person is in trouble.
(Eccles. 8:5-6)

A wise person chooses the right road;
a fool takes the wrong one.
(Eccles. 10:2)

## RIGHTEOUS(NESS)

"The righteous keep moving forward,
and those with clean hands
become stronger and stronger."
(Job 17:9)

"Can a person do anything to help God?
Can even a wise person be helpful to him?
Is it any advantage to the Almighty
if you are righteous?
Would it be any gain to him
if you were perfect?"(Eliphaz)
(Job 22:2-3)

"Everything I did was honest.
Righteousness covered me like a robe,
and I wore justice like a turban."
(Job 29:14)

"Do you think it is right for you to claim,
'I am righteous before God?'
For you also ask, 'What's in it for me?
What's the use of living a righteous life?'"(Elihu)
(Job 35:2-3)

"Let me go on, and I will show you the truth.
For I have not finished defending God!
I will present profound arguments
for the righteousness of my Creator."(Elihu)
(Job 36:23)

The Lord judges the nations.
Declare me righteous, O Lord,
for I am innocent, O Most High!
End the evil of those who are wicked,
and defend the righteous.
For you look deep within the mind and heart,
O Righteous God.
(Psalm 7:8-9)

The foundations of law and order have collapsed.
What can the righteous do?
But the Lord is in his holy Temple;
the Lord still rules from heaven.
He watches everyone closely,
The Lord examines both the righteous and the wicked.
He hates those who love violence.
(Psalm 11:3-5)

For the righteous Lord loves justice.
The virtuous will see his face.
(Psalm 11:7)

Because I am righteous, I will see you.
When I awake,
I will see you face to face and be satisfied.
(Psalm 17:15)

Our children will also serve him.
Future generations will hear
about the wonders of the Lord.
His righteous acts will be told
to those not yet born.
They will hear about everything he has done.
(Psalm 22:30-31)

The righteous person faces many troubles,
but the Lord comes to the rescue each time.
For the Lord protects the bones of the righteous;
not one of them is broken.
Calamity will surely overtake the wicked,
and those who hate the righteous
will be punished.
(Psalm 34:19-21)

Your righteousness
is like the mighty mountains,
your justice like the ocean depths.
You care for people and animals alike, O Lord.
(Psalm 36:6)

Your righteousness, O God,
reaches to the highest heavens.
You have done such wonderful things.
Who can compare with you, O God?
(Psalm 71:19)

I will tell about your righteous deeds
all day long,
for everyone who tried to hurt me
has been shamed and humiliated.
(Psalm 71:24)

Unfailing love and truth have met together.
Righteousness and peace have kissed!
Truth springs up from the earth,
and righteousness smiles down from heaven.
(Psalm 85:10-11)

Righteousness goes as a herald before him,
preparing the way for his steps.
(Psalm 85:13)

Righteousness and justice
are the foundation of your throne.
Unfailing love and truth
walk before you as attendants.
(Psalm 89:14)

The heavens proclaim his righteousness.
Every nation sees his glory.
(Psalm 97:6)

The Lord has announced his victory
and has revealed his righteousness
to every nation!
(Psalm 98:2)

Mighty King, Lover of justice,
you have established fairness.
You have acted
with justice and righteousness throughout Israel.
(Psalm 99:4)

The Lord gives righteousness and justice
to all who are treated unfairly.
(Psalm 103:6)

How amazing are the deeds of the Lord!
All who delight in him should ponder them.
Everything he does
reveals his glory and majesty.
His righteousness never fails.
(Psalm 111:2-3)

Good comes to those who lend generously
and conduct their business fairly.
Such people will not be overcome by evil.
Those who are righteous
will be long remembered.
(Psalm 112:5-6)

As I learn your righteous regulations,
I will thank you by living as I should!
(Psalm 119:7)

O Lord, you are righteous,
and your regulations are fair.
(Psalm 119:137)

Surely, righteous people are praising your name;
the godly will live in your presence.
(Psalm 140:13)

Here my prayer, O Lord;
listen to my plea.
Answer me because you are faithful and righteous.
(Psalm 143:1)

Everyone will share
the story of your wonderful goodness;
they will sing with joy about your righteousness.
(Psalm 145:7)

The Lord is righteous in everything he does;
he is filled with kindness.
(Psalm 145:17)

The way of the righteous
is like the first gleam of dawn,
which shines ever brighter
until the full light of dawn.
But the way of the wicked is like total darkness.
They have no idea what they are stumbling over.
(Prov. 4:18-19)

"I(Wisdom) walk in righteousness,
in paths of justice.
Those who love me inherit wealth.
I will fill their treasuries."
(Prov. 8:20-21)

Instruct the wise and they will be even wiser.
Teach the righteous,
and they will learn even more.
(Prov. 9:9)

With their words,
the godless destroy their friends,
but knowledge will rescue the righteous.
(Prov. 11:9)

If the righteous are rewarded here on earth,
what will happen to wicked sinners?
(Prov. 11:31)

Trouble chases sinners,
while blessings reward the righteous.
(Prov. 13:21)

The Righteous One knows what is going on
in the homes of the wicked;
he will bring disaster on them.
(Prov. 21:12)

Whoever pursues righteousness and unfailing love
will find life, righteousness and honor.
(Prov. 21:21)

Evil people are trapped by sin,
but the righteous escape,
shouting for joy.
(Prov. 29:6)

# Chapter 22

# S

## SELF-CONTROL

A person without self-control
is like a city with broken-down walls.
(Prov. 25:28)

## SHORT-TEMPERED

Short-tempered people do foolish things,
and schemers are hated.
(Prov. 14:17)

## SILENT

"If only you could be silent!
That's the wisest thing you could do."
(Job 13:5)

Don't sin by letting anger control you.
Think about it overnight and remain silent.
(Psalm 4:4)

I pray to you, O Lord, my rock.
Do not turn a deaf ear to me.
For if you are silent,
I might as well give up and die.
(Psalm 28:1)

You have turned my mourning
into joyful dancing.
You have taken away my clothes of mourning
and clothed me with joy,
that I might sing praises to you
and not be silent.
O Lord, my God,
I will give you thanks forever!
(Psalm 30:11-12)

O Lord, you know all about this.
Do not stay silent.
Do not abandon me now, O Lord.
Wake up! Rise to my defense!
Take up my case,
my God and my Lord.
(Psalm 35:22-23)

O God, do not be silent!
Do not be deaf.
Do not be quiet, O God.
(Psalm 83:1

## SIMPLETON

Only simpletons believe everything they're told!
The prudent carefully consider their steps.
(Prov. 14:15)

A prudent person foresees danger
and takes precautions.
The simpleton goes blindly on
and suffers the consequences.
(Prov. 22:3)

## SIN (SINNER)

Job stood up and tore his robe in grief.
Then he shaved his head
and fell to the ground to worship.
He said,
"I came naked from my mother's womb,
and I will be naked when I leave.
The Lord gave me what I had,
and the Lord has taken it away.
Praise the name of the Lord!"
In all of this, Job did not sin by blaming God.
(Job 1:20-22)

"But consider the joy of those corrected by God!
Do not despise the discipline of the Almighty
when you sin. For though he wounds,
he also bandages.
He strikes, but his hands also heal."(Eliphaz)
(Job 5:17-18)

"If I have sinned, what have I done to you,
O watcher of all humanity?
Why make me your target?
Am I a burden to you?
Why not just forgive my sin
and take away my guilt?
For soon I will lie down in the dust and die.
When you look for me,
I will be gone."
(Job 7:20-21)

"Your children must have sinned against him,
so their punishment was well deserved."
(Job 8:4)

"Is your lifetime only as long as ours?
Is your life so short that you must quickly
probe for my guilt and search for my sin?
Although you know I am not guilty,
no one can rescue me from your hands."
(Job 10:5-7)

"Yet your real motive—your true intent—
was to watch me, and if I sinned,
you would not forgive my guilt.
If I am guilty, too bad for me;
and even if I am innocent,
I can't hold my head high,
because I am filled with shame and misery."
(Job 10:13-15)

"If only you would prepare your heart
and lift up your hands to him in prayer!
Get rid of your sins,
and leave all iniquity behind you.
Then your face will brighten with innocence.
You will be strong and free of fear."(Zophar)
(Job 11:13-15)

"Now summon me, and I will answer!
Or let me speak to you, and you reply.
Tell me, what have I done wrong?
Show me my rebellion and my sin."
(Job 13:22-23)

"You write bitter accusations against me
and bring up all the sins of my youth.
You put my feet in stocks.
You examine all my paths.
You trace all my footprints.
I waste away like rotting wood,
like a moth-eaten coat."
(Job 13:26-28)

"Can the dead live again?
If so, this would give me hope
through all my years of struggle,
and I would eagerly await the release of death.
You would call and I would answer,
and you would yearn for me,
your handiwork.
For then you would guard my steps,
instead of watching for my sins."
(Job 14:14-16)

"Have you no fear of God,
no reverence for him?
Your sins are telling your mouth what to say.
Your words are based on clever deception.
Your own mouth condemns you, not I.
Your own lips testify against you."(Eliphaz)
(Job 15:4-6)

"People jeer and laugh at me.
They slap my cheek in contempt.
A mob gathers against me.
God has handed me over to sinners.
He has tossed me
into the hands of the wicked."
(Job 16:10-11)

"Even if I have sinned,
that is my concern, not yours.
You think you're better than I am,
using my humiliation as evidence of my sin.
But it is God who has wronged me,
capturing me in his net."
(Job 19:4-6)

"'Well,' you say, 'at least God will punish
their(wicked) children!'
But I say he should punish the ones who sin,
so that they understand his judgment."
(Job 21:19)

"You will tell me of rich and wicked people
whose houses have vanished because of their sins.
But ask those who have been around,
and they will tell you the truth.
Evil people are spared in times of calamity
and are allowed to escape disaster."
(Job 21:28-30)

"Is it because you're so pious
that he accuses you
and brings judgment against you?
No, it's because of your wickedness!
There's no limit to your sins.
For example,
you must have lent money to your friend
and demanded clothing as security.
Yes, you stripped him to the bone.
You must have refused water for the thirsty
and food for the hungry."(Eliphaz)
(Job 22:4-7)

"Let God weigh me on the scales of justice,
for he knows my integrity.
If I have strayed from his pathway,
or if my heart has lusted
for what my eyes have seen,
or if I am guilty of any other sin,
then let someone else
eat the crops I have planted.
Let all that I have planted be uprooted."
(Job 31:6-8)

"If my heart has been seduced by a woman,
or if I have lusted for my neighbor's wife,
then let my wife belong to another man;
let other men sleep with her.
For lust is a shameful sin,
a crime that should be punished."
(Job 31:9-11)

"Have I ever rejoiced
when disaster struck my enemies,
or become excited when harm came their way?
No, I have never sinned by cursing anyone
or by asking for revenge."
(Job 31:29-30)
"Listen to me, you who have understanding.
Everyone knows that God doesn't sin!
The Almighty can do no wrong.
He repays people according to their deeds.
He treats people as they deserve."(Elihu)
(Job 34:10-11)

"Why don't people say to God, 'I have sinned,
but I will sin no more'?
Or, 'I don't know what evil I have done—tell me.
If I have done wrong, I will stop at once'?
Must God tailor his justice to your demands?"(Elihu)
(Job 34:31-33)

"Job, you deserve the maximum penalty
for the wicked way you have talked,
for you have added rebellion to your sin;
you show no respect,
and you speak many angry words against God."(Elihu)
(Job 34:36-37)

"If you sin, how does that affect God?
Even if you sin again and again,
what effect will it have on him?
If you are good,
is this some great gift to him?
What could you possibly give him?
No, your sins affect only people like yourself,
and your good deeds
also affect only humans."(Elihu)
(Job 35:6-8)

"You say he does not respond
to sinners with anger
and is not greatly concerned about wickedness.
But you are talking nonsense, Job.
You have spoken like a fool."(Elihu)
(Job 35:15-16)

"God is leading you away from danger, Job,
to a place free from distress.
He is setting your table
with the best food.
But you are obsessed
with whether the godless will be judged.
Don't worry,
judgment and justice will be upheld.
But watch out,
or you may be seduced by wealth.
Don't let yourself be bribed into sin."(Elihu)
(Job 36:16-18)

Oh, the joys of those
who do not follow the advice of the wicked,
or stand around with sinners,
or join in with mockers.
(Psalm 1:1)

They(wicked) will be condemned
at the time of judgment.
Sinners will have no place among the godly.
For the Lord watches over the path of the godly,
but the path of the wicked leads to destruction.
(Psalm 1:5-6)

Don't sin by letting anger control you.
Think about it overnight and remain silent.
(Psalm 4:4)

O God,
you take no pleasure in wickedness;
you cannot tolerate the sins of the wicked.
Therefore the proud
may not stand in your presence,
for you hate all who do evil.
(Psalm 5:4-5)

You have tested my thoughts
and examined my heart in the night.
You have scrutinized me
and found nothing wrong.
I am determined not to sin in what I say.
(Psalm 17:3)

I have followed all his regulations;
I have never abandoned his decrees.
I am blameless before God;
I have kept myself from sin.
(Psalm 18:22-23)

Keep your servant from deliberate sins!
Don't let them control me.
Then I will be free of guilt
and innocent of great sin.
(Psalm 19:13)

For the honor of your name, O Lord,
forgive my many, many sins.
Who are those who fear the Lord?
He will show them the path they should choose.
(Psalm 25:11-12)

Don't let me suffer the fate of sinners.
Don't condemn me along with murderers.
Their hands are dirty with evil schemes,
and they constantly take bribes.
(Psalm 26:9-10)

Oh, what joy for those
whose disobedience is forgiven,
whose sin is put out of sight.
(Psalm 32:1)

Finally, I confessed all my sins to you
and stopped trying to hide my guilt.
I said to myself,
"I will confess my rebelion to the Lord."
And you forgave me!
All my guilt is gone.
(Psalm 32:5)

Sin whispers to the wicked,
deep within their hearts.
They have no fear of God at all.
In their blind conceit,
They cannot see how wicked they really are.
(Psalm 36:1-2)

O Lord, don't rebuke me in your anger
or discipline me in your rage!
Your arrows have struck deep,
and your blows are crushing me.
Because of your anger,
my whole body is sick;
my health is broken because of my sins.
My guilt overwhelms me—
it is a burden too heavy to bear.
But I confess my sins;
I am deeply sorry for what I have done.
(Psalm 38:1-4, 18)

I said to myself, "I will watch what I do
and not sin in what I say.
I will hold my tongue
when the ungodly are around me."
(Psalm 39:1)

When you discipline us for our sins,
you consume like a moth
what is precious to us.
Each of us is but a breath.
(Psalm 39:11)

For troubles surround me—
too many to count!
My sins pile up so high I can't see my way out.
They outnumber the hairs on my head.
I have lost all courage.
Please Lord, rescue me!
Come quickly, Lord, and help me.
(Psalm 40:12-13)

Have mercy on me, O God,
because of yor unfailing love.
Because of your great compassion,
blot out the stain of my sins.
Wash me clean from my guilt.
Purify me from my sin.
For I recognize my rebellion;
it haunts me day and night.
Against you, and you alone, have I sinned;
I have done what is evil in your sight.
You will be proved right in what you say,
and your judgment against me is just.
For I was born a sinner—
yes, from the moment my mother conceived me.
(Psalm 51:1-5)

Don't keep looking at my sins.
Remove the stain of my guilt.
Create in me a clean heart, O God.
Renew a loyal spirit within me.
(Psalm 51:9-10)

If I had not confessed the sin in my heart,
the Lord would not have listened.
But God did listen!
He paid attention to my prayer.
(Psalm 66:18-19)

Do not hold us guilty
for the sins of our ancestors!
Let your compassion quickly meet our needs,
for we are on the brink of despair.
Help us, O God of our salvation!
Help us for the glory of your name.
Save us and forgive our sins,
for the honor of your name.
(Psalm 79:8-9)

Lord,
you poured out blessings on your land!
You restored the fortunes of Israel.
You forgave the guilt of your people—
yes, you covered all our sins.
(Psalm 85:1-2)

Let all that I am praise the Lord;
may I never forget the good things
he does for me.
He forgives all my sins
and heals all my diseases.
(Psalm 103:2-3)

He does not punish us for all our sins;
he does not deal harshly with us,
as we deserve.
For his unfailing love
toward those who fear him is as great as
the height of the heavens above the earth.
He has removed our sins as far from us
as the east is from the west.
(Psalm 103:10-12)

Lord, if you kept a record of our sins,
who, O Lord, could ever survive?
But you offer forgiveness,
that we might learn to fear you.
(Psalm 130:3-4)

My child, if sinners entice you,
turn your back on them!
(Prov. 1:10)

An evil man is held captive by his own sins;
they are ropes that catch and hold him.
(Prov. 5:22)

The earnings of the godly enhance their lives,
but evil people squander their money on sin.
(Prov. 10:16)

The godly are directed by honesty;
the wicked fall beneath their load of sin.
(Prov. 11:5)

Godliness guards the path of the blameless,
but the evil are misled by sin.
(Prov. 13:6)

Trouble chases sinners,
while blessings reward the righteous.
(Prov. 13:21)

It is a sin to belittle one's neighbor;
blessed are those who help the poor.
(Prov. 14:21)

Godliness makes a nation great,
but sin is a disgrace to any people.
(Prov. 14:34)

Unfailing love and faithfulness
make atonement for sin.
By fearing the Lord, people avoid evil.
(Prov. 16:6)

Haughty eyes, a proud heart
and evil actions are all sin.
(Prov. 21:4)

Don't envy sinners
but always continue to fear the Lord.
(Prov. 23:17)

People who conceal their sins will not prosper,
but if they confess and turn from them,
they will receive mercy.
(Prov. 28:13)

## SUFFER (SUFFERING)

When three of Job's friends heard of the tragedy
he had suffered, they got together and traveled
from their homes to comfort and console him.
Their names were Eliphaz the Temanite,
Bildad the Shuhite, and Zophar the Naamathite.
When they saw Job from a distance, they
scarcely recognized him. Wailing loudly,
they tore their robes and threw dust into the air
over their heads to show their grief.
Then they sat on the ground with him for
seven days and nights. No one said a word
to Job, for they saw that his suffering was too
great for words.
(Job 2:11-13)

"He does great things too marvelous
to understand. He performs countless
miracles. He gives rain for the earth
and water for the fields.
He gives prosperity to the poor
and protects those who suffer."(Eliphaz)
(Job 5:9-11)

"I would rather be strangled—
rather die than suffer like this.
I hate my life
and don't want to go on living.
Oh, leave me alone
for my few remaining days."
(Job 7:15-16)

"I could say the same things
if you were in my place.
I could spout off criticism
and shake my head at you.
But if it were me,
I would encourage you.
I would try to take away your grief.
Instead, I suffer if I defend myself,
and I suffer no less
if I refuse to speak."
(Job 16:4-6)

"My heart is troubled and restless.
Days of suffering torment me.
I walk in gloom, without sunlight.
I stand in the public square and cry for help."
(Job 30:27-28)

"So let us discern for ourselves what is right;
let us learn together what is good.
For Job also said, 'I am innocent,
but God has taken away my rights.
I am innocent, but they call me a liar.
My suffering is incurable,
though I have not sinned.'"(Elihu)
(Job 34:4-6)

"For the godless are full of resentment.
Even when he punishes them,
they refuse to cry out to him for help.
They die when they are young,
after wasting their lives in immoral living.
But by means of their suffering,
he rescues those who suffer.
For he gets their attention through adversity."(Elihu)
(Job 36:13-15)

"Be on guard!
Turn back from evil,
for God sent this suffering
to keep you from a life of evil."(Elihu)
(Job 36:21)

Sing praises to the Lord
who reigns in Jerusalem.
Tell the world about his unforgettable deeds.
For he who avenges murder,
cares for the helpless.
He does not ignore
the cries of those who suffer.
(Psalm 22:23-24)

I am suffering and in pain.
Rescue me, O God, by your saving power.
Then I will praise God's name with singing,
and I will honor him with thanksgiving.
(Psalm 69:29-30)

You have allowed me
to suffer much hardship,
but you will restore me to life again
and lift me up
from the depths of the earth.
You will restore me to even greater honor
and comfort me once again.
(Psalm 71:20-21)

My suffering was good for me,
for it taught me
to pay attention to your decrees.
Your instructions are more valuable to me
than millions in gold and silver.
(Psalm 119:71-72)

Your word is a lamp to guide my feet
and a light for my path.
I've promised it once,
and I'll promise it again:
I will obey your righteous regulations.
I have suffered much, O Lord;
restore my life again as you promised.
(Psalm 119:105-107)

Look upon my suffering and rescue me,
for I have not forgotten your instructions.
Argue my case;
take my side!
Protect my life as you promised.
(Psalm 119:153-154)

Lord,
remember David and all that he suffered.
He made a solemn promise to the Lord.
He vowed to the Mighty One of Israel:
"I will not go home;
I will not let myself rest.
I will not let my eyes sleep
nor close my eyelids in slumber,
until I find a place
to build a house for the Lord,
a sanctuary for the Mighty One of Israel."
(Psalm 132:1-5)

# Chapter 23

# T

## TALK (TONGUE)

Too much talk leads to sin.
Be sensible and keep your mouth shut.
(Prov. 10:29)

A fool's proud talk becomes a rod that beats him,
but the words of the wise keep them safe.
(Prov. 14:3)

The tongue can bring death or life;
those who love to talk will reap the consequences.
(Prov. 18:21)

Watch your tongue and keep your mouth shut
and you will stay out of trouble.
(Prov. 21:23)

## TIME FOR EVERYTHING

For everything there is a season,
a time for every activity under heaven.
A time to be born and a time to die.
A time to plant and a time to harvest.
A time to kill and a time to heal.
A time to tear down and a time to build up.
A time to cry and a time to laugh.
A time to grieve and a time to dance.
A time to scatter stones and a time to gather stones.
A time to embrace and a time to turn away.
A time to search and a time to quit searching.
A time to keep and a time to throw away.
A time to tear and a time to mend.
A time to be quiet and a time to speak.
A time to love and a time to hate.
A time for war and a time for peace.
(Eccles. 3:1-8)

## TOMORROW

Don't brag about tomorrow,
since you don't know what the day will bring.
(Prov. 27:1)

## TRAP

If you set a trap for others,
you will get caught in it yourself.
If you roll a boulder down on others.
it will crush you instead.
(Prov. 26:27)

I discovered that a seductive woman
is a trap more bitter than death.
Her passion is a snare,
and her soft hands are chains.
Those who are pleasing to God
will escape her,
but sinners will be caught in her snare.
(Eccles. 7:26)

## TROUBLE

"Let those who are experts at cursing—
whose cursing could rouse Leviathan—
curse that day(day of birth).
Let its morning stars remain dark.
Let it hope for light, but in vain;
may it never see the morning light.
Curse that day
for failing to shut my mother's womb,
for letting me be born
to see all this trouble."
(Job 3: 8-10)

"Why wasn't I buried like a stillborn child,
like a baby who never lives to see the light?
For in death the wicked cause no trouble,
and the weary are at rest."
(Job 3:16-17)

"What I always feared has happened to me.
What I dreaded has come true.
I have no peace, no quietness.
I have no rest; only trouble comes."
(Job 3:25-26)

"Stop and think!
Do the innocent die?
When have the upright been destroyed?
My experience shows
that those who plant trouble and cultivate evil
will harvest the same."(Eliphaz)
(Job 4:7-8)

"But evil does not spring from the soil,
and trouble does not sprout
from the earth.
People are born for trouble
as readily as sparks fly up from a fire."(Eliphaz)
(Job 5:6-7)

"If my misery could be weighed
and my troubles be put on the scales,
they would outweigh
all the sands of the sea.
That is why I spoke impulsively."
(Job 6:2-3)

"People who are at ease
mock those in trouble.
They give a push to people who are stumbling."
(Job 12:5)

"How frail is humanity!
How short is life, how full of trouble!
We blossom like a flower and then wither.
Like a passing shadow, we quickly disappear."
(Job 14:1-2)

"They(people who die early) never know
if their children grow up in honor
or sink to insignificance.
They suffer painfully;
their life is full of trouble."
(Job 14:21-22)

"Terrors surround the wicked
and trouble them at every step."(Bildad)
(Job 18:11)

"In the midst of plenty,
they(wicked) will run into trouble
and be overcome by misery.
May God give them a bellyful of trouble.
May God rain down his anger upon them."(Zophar)
(Job 20:22-23)

"They(wicked) spend their days in prosperity,
then go down to the grave in peace.
And yet they say to God, 'Go away.
We want no part of you and your ways.
Who is the Almighty,
and why should we obey him?
What good will it do us to pray?'
(They think their prosperity
is of their own doing, but I will have
nothing to do with that kind of thinking.)
Yet the light of the wicked
never seems to be extinguished.
Do they ever have trouble?
Does God distribute sorrows to them in anger?"
(Job 21:13-17)

"Surely, no one would turn against the needy
when they cry for help in their trouble.
Did I not weep for those in trouble?
Was I not deeply grieved for the needy?
So I looked for good, but evil came instead.
I waited for the light, but darkness fell."
(Job 30:24-26)

Answer me when I call to you, O God,
who declares me innocent.
Free me from my troubles.
Have mercy on me and hear my prayer.
(Psalm 4:1)

The wicked conceive evil;
they are pregnant with trouble
and give birth to lies.
They dig a deep pit to trap others,
then fall into it themselves.
The trouble they make for others
backfires on them.
The violence they plan
falls on their own heads.
(Psalm 7:14-16)

The Lord is a shelter for the oppressed,
a refuge in times of trouble.
(Psalm 9:9)

O Lord, why do you stand so far away?
Why do you hide when I am in trouble?
(Psalm 10:1)

The wicked are too proud to seek God.
They seem to think that God is dead.
Yet, they succeed in everything they do.
They do not see
your punishment awaiting them.
They sneer at all their enemies.
They think, "Nothing bad will ever happen to us!
We will be free of trouble forever!"
Their mouths are full of
cursing, lies and threats.
Trouble and evil
are on the tips of their tongues.
(Psalm 10:4-7)

Why do the wicked
get away with despising God?
They think, "God will never call us to account."
But you see the trouble and grief they cause.
You take note of it and punish them.
The helpless put their trust in you.
You defend the orphans.
(Psalm10:13-14)

The godly people in the land
are my true heroes!
I take pleasure in them.
Troubles multiply for those
who chase after other gods.
(Psalm 16:3-4)

In times of trouble,
may the Lord answer your cry.
May the name of the God of Jacob
keep you safe from all harm.
(Psalm 20:1)

Do not stay so far from me,
for trouble is near,
and no one else can help us.
(Psalm 22:11)

My problems go from bad to worse.
Oh, save me from them all!
Feel my pain and see my trouble.
Forgive all my sins.
(Psalm 25:17-18)

I will be glad and rejoice
in your unfailing love,
for you have seen my troubles,
and you care about the anguish of my soul.
(Psalm 31:7)

For you are my hiding place;
you protect me from trouble.
you surround me with songs of victory.
(Psalm 32:7)

The righteous person faces many troubles,
but the Lord comes to the rescue each time.
(Psalm 34:19)

Wake up! Rise to my defense!
Take up my case, my God and my Lord.
Declare me not guilty, O Lord my God,
for you give justice.
Don't let my enemies
laugh about me in my troubles.
(Psalm 35:23-24)

The Lord rescues the godly;
he is their fortress in times of trouble.
(Psalm 37:39)

Oh, the joys of those
who are kind to the poor!
The Lord rescues them
when they are in trouble.
(Psalm 41:1)

God is our refuge and our strength,
always ready to help in times of trouble.
(Psalm 46:1)

Why should I fear when trouble comes,
when enemies surround me?
They trust in their wealth
and boast of great riches.
Yet they cannot redeem themselves from death
by paying a ransom to God.
(Psalm 49:5-7)

"Make thankfulness your sacrifice to God,
and keep the vows you made
to the Most High.
Then call on me when you are in trouble,
and I will rescue,
and you will give me glory."
(Psalm 50:14-15)

I will sacrifice a voluntary offering to you;
I will praise your name, O Lord,
for it is good.
For you have rescued me from my troubles
and helped me to triumph over my enemies.
(Psalm 54:6-7)

Listen to my prayer, O God.
Do not ignore my cry for help!
Please listen and answer me,
for I am overwhelmed by my troubles.
(Psalm 55:1-2)

Please, God, rescue me!
Come quickly, Lord, and help me.
May those who try to kill me
be humiliated and put to shame.
May those who take delight in my trouble
be turned back in disgrace.
(Psalm 70:1-2)

But as for me, I almost lost my footing.
My feet were slipping
and I was almost gone.
For I envied the proud
when I saw them prosper
despite their wickedness.
They seem to live such painless lives;
their bodies are so healthy and strong.
They don't have troubles like other people;
they're not plagued with problems
like everyone else.
(Psalm 73:2-5)

When I was I deep trouble,
I searched for the Lord.
All night long I prayed,
with hands lifted toward heaven,
but my soul was not comforted.
(Psalm 77:2)

Now hear my prayer;
listen to my cry.
For my life is full of troubles,
and death draws n ear.
I am as good as dead,
like a strong man with no strength left.
(Psalm 88:2-4)

Seventy years are given to us!
Some even live to eighty.
But even the best years
are filled with pain and trouble;
soon they disappear, and we fly away.
(Psalm 90:10)

The Lord says,
"I will rescue those who love me
I will protect those who trust in my name.
When they call on me, I will answer;
I will be with them in trouble.
I will rescue and honor them."
(Psalm 91:14-15)

Remember your promise to me;
it is my only hope.
Your promise revives me;
it comforts me in all my troubles.
(Psalm 119:49-50)

I took my troubles to the Lord.
I cried out to him,
and he answered my prayer.(Psalm 120:1)
What are worthless and wicked people like?
They are constant liars,
signaling their deceit
with a wink of the eye,
a nudge of the foot,
or the wiggle of the fingers.
Their perverted hearts plot evil,
and they constantly stir up trouble.
(Prov. 6:12-14)

People who wink at wrong cause trouble,
but a bold reproof promotes peace.
(Prov. 10:10)

The godly are rescued from trouble,
and it falls on the wicked instead.
(Prov. 11:8)

The wicked are trapped by their own words
but the godly escape such trouble.
(Prov. 12:13)

Scoundrels create trouble;
their words are a destructive blaze.
(Prov. 16:27)

Don't envy evil people
or desire their company.
For their hearts plot violence,
and their words always stir up trouble.
(Prov. 24:1)

Putting confidence in an unreliable person
in times of trouble,
is like chewing with a broken tooth
or walking on a lame foot.
(Prov. 25:19)

Blessed are those who fear to do wrong,
but the stubborn
are headed for serious trouble.
(Prov. 28:14)

## TROUBLEMAKER

A troublemaker plants seeds of strife;
gossip separates the best of friends.
(Prov. 16:28)

## TRUST

"They(wicked) will not escape the darkness.
The burning sun will wither their shoots,
and the breath of God will destroy them.
Let them no longer fool themselves
by trusting in empty riches, for emptiness
will be their only reward." (Eliphaz)
(Job 15:30-31)

Offer sacrifices in the right spirit,
and trust the Lord.
Many people say,
"Who will show us better times?"
Let your face smile on us, Lord.
(Psalm 4:5-6)

Do you see the trouble
and grief they(wicked) cause.
You take note of it and punish them.
The helpless put their trust in you.
You defend the orphans.
(Psalm 10:14)

I trust in the Lord for protection.
So why do you say to me,
"Fly like a bird to the mountains for safety."
(Psalm 11:1)

Our ancestors trusted in you,
and you rescued them.
They cried out to you and were saved.
They trusted in you
and were never disgraced.
(Psalm 22:4-5)

O Lord, I give my life to you.
I trust in you, my God!
Do not let me be disgraced,
or let my enemies rejoice in my defeat.
No one who trust in you
will ever be disgraced,
because disgrace comes to those
who try to deceive others.
(Psalm 25:1-3)

Declare me innocent, O Lord,
for I have acted in integrity.
I have trusted in the Lord without wavering.
(Psalm 26:1)

The Lord is my strength and shield.
I trust him with all my heart.
He helps me and my heart is filled with joy.
I burst out in songs of thanksgiving.
(Psalm 28:7)

I entrust my spirit into your hand.
Rescue me, Lord, for you are a faithful God.
I hate those who worship worthless idols.
(Psalm 31:5-6)

Many sorrows come to the wicked,
but unfailing love
surrounds those who trust the Lord.
(Psalm 32:10)

For the word of the Lord holds true,
and we can trust everything he does.
(Psalm 33:4)

Even strong young lions
sometimes go hungry,
but those who trust in the Lord
will lack no good thing.
(Psalm 34:10)

Trust in the Lord and do good.
Then you will live safely
in the land and prosper.
Take delight in the Lord,
and he will give you your heart's desires.
Commit everything you do to the Lord.
Trust him, and he will help you.
(Psalm 37:3-5)

He has given me a new song to sing,
a hymn of praise to our God.
Many will see what he has done
and be amazed.
They will put their trust in the Lord.
Oh, the joys of those who trust the Lord,
who have no confidence in the proud
or in those who worship idols.
(Psalm 40:3-4)

Even my best friend,
the one I trusted completely,
the one who shared my food,
has turned against me.
(Psalm 41:9)

They(enemies) trust in their wealth
and boast of great riches.
Yet they cannot redeem themselves from death
by paying a ransom to God.
(Psalm 49:6-7)

Look what happens to mighty warriors
who do not trust in God.
They trust their wealth instead,
and grow more and more bold
in their wickedness.
But I am like an olive tree,
thriving in the house of God.
I will always trust in God's unfailing love.
(Psalm 52:7-8)

But when I am afraid,
I will put my trust in you.
I praise God for what he has promised.
I trust in God,
so why should I be afraid?
What can mere mortals do to me?
(Psalm 56:3-4)

O my people, trust in him at all times.
Pour out your heart to him,
for God is our refuge.
(Psalm 62:8)

O Lord, you alone are my hope.
I've trusted you, O Lord, from childhood.
(Psalm 71:5)

O Lord of Heaven's Armies,
what joy for those who trust in you.
(Psalm 84:12)

Protect me, for I am devoted to you.
Save me, for I serve you and trust you.
You are my God.
(Psalm 86:2)

The Lord says,
"I will rescue those who love me.
I will protect those who trust in my name."
(Psalm 91:14)

All you who fear the Lord, trust the Lord!
He is your helper and your shield.
(Psalm 115:11)

It is better to take refuge in the Lord
than to trust in people.
It is better to take refuge in the Lord
than to trust in princes.
(Psalm 118:8-9)

Lord, give me your unfailing love,
the salvation that you promised me.
Then I can answer those who taunt me,
for I trust I your word.
(Psalm 119:41-42)

Those who trust in the Lord
are as secure as Mount Zion;
they will not be defeated
but will endure forever.
(Psalm 125:1)

Trust in the Lord with all your heart;
do not depend on your own understanding.
Seek his will in all you do,
and he will show you which path to take.
(Prov. 3:5-6)

Those who listen to instruction will prosper;
those who trust the Lord will be joyful.
(Prov. 16:20)

Trusting a fool to convey a message
is like cutting off one's feet or drinking poison.
(Prov. 26:6)

Greed causes fighting;
trusting the Lord leads to prosperity.
Those who trust their own insight are foolish,
but anyone who walks in wisdom is safe.
(Prov. 28:25-26)

## TRUTH (TRUE)

"If only God would speak;
if only he would tell you what he thinks!
If only he would tell you the secrets of wisdom,
for true wisdom is not a simple matter.
Listen! God is doubtless punishing you
far less than you deserve!"(Zophar)
(Job 11:5-6)

"But true wisdom and power are found in God;
counsel and understanding are his.
What he destroys cannot be rebuilt.
When he puts someone in prison
there is no escape."
(Job 12:13-14)

"But ask those who have been around,
and they will tell you the truth.
Evil people are spared
in times of calamity
and are allowed to escape disaster."
(Job 21:29-30)

"And this is what he says to all humanity:
'The fear of the Lord is true wisdom;
to forsake evil is real understanding.'"
(Job 28:28)

"I speak with all sincerity;
I speak the truth.
For the Spirit of God has made me,
and the breath of the Almighty gives me life."(Elihu)
(Job 33:3)

"Let us go on,
and I will show you the truth.
For I have not finished defending God!
I will present profound arguments
for the righteousness of my Creator.
I am telling you nothing but the truth,
for I am a man of great knowledge.
God is mighty,
but he does not despise anyone!
He is mighty in both power and understanding.
He does not let the wicked live
but gives justice to the afflicted."(Elihu)
(Job 36:2-6)

The godly people in the land
are my true heroes!
I take pleasure in them.
(Psalm 16:3)

God's way is perfect.
All the Lord's promises prove true.
He is a shield
for all who look to him for protection.
(Psalm 18:30)

Reverence for the Lord
is pure, lasting forever.
The laws of the Lord are true;
each one is fair.
They are more desirable than gold,
even the finest gold.
They are sweeter than honey,
even honey dripping from the comb.
(Psalm 19:9-10)

Lead me by your truth and teach me,
for you are the God who saves me.
All day long I put my hope in you.
(Psalm 25:5)

Put me on trial, Lord,
and cross-examine me.
Test my motives and my heart.
For I am always aware
of your unfailing love,
and I have lived according to your truth.
(Psalm 26:2-3)

For the word of the Lord holds true,
and we can trust everything he does.
(Psalm 33:4)

Send out your light and your truth;
let them guide me.
Let them lead me to your holy mountain,
to the place where you live.
(Psalm 43:3)

Why do you boast
about your crimes, great warrior?
Don't you realize God's justice continues forever?
All day long you plot destruction.
Your tongue cuts like a sharp razor;
you're an expert at telling lies.
You love evil more than good
and lies more than truth.
You love to destroy others
with your words, you liar!
But God will strike you down once and for all.
(Psalm 52:1-5)

Unfailing love and truth have met together.
Righteousness and peace have kissed!
Truth springs up from the earth,
and righteousness smiles down from heaven.
(Psalm 85:10-11)

Teach me your ways, O Lord,
that I may live according to your truth.
Grant me purity of heart,
so that I may honor you.
(Psalm 86:11)

Righteousness and justice
are the foundation of your throne.
Unfailing love and truth
walk before you as attendants.
(Psalm 89:14)

Let the heavens be glad,
and the earth rejoice!
Let the sea and everything in it
shout his praise!
Let the fields and their crops
burst out with joy!
Let the trees of the forest
rustle with praise before the Lord,
for he is coming!
He is coming to judge the earth.
He will judge the world with justice,
and the nations with his truth.
(Psalm 96:11-13)

Open my eyes to see
the wonderful truths in your instructions.
(Psalm 119:18)

Do not snatch your word of truth from me,
for your regulations
are my only hope.
I will keep on obeying your instructions
forever and ever.
(Psalm 119:43-44)

Arrogant people smear me with lies,
but in truth I obey your commandments
with all my heart.
(Psalm 119:69)

Your regulations remain true to this day,
for everything serves your plans.
(Psalm 119:91)

My eyes strain to see your rescue,
to see the truth of your promise fulfilled.
(Psalm 119 :123)

Your justice is eternal,
and your instructions are perfectly true.
(Psalm 119:142)

Lawless people are coming to attack me;
they live far from your instructions.
But you are near, O Lord,
and all your commands are true.
(Psalm 119:150-151)

The very essence of your words is truth;
all your just regulations will stand forever.
(Psalm 119:160)

The Lord is close to all who call on him,
yes, to all who call him in truth.
(Psalm 145:18)

Listen to me!
For I(Wisdom) have important things
to tell you.
Everything I say is right,
for I speak the truth
and detest every kind of deception.
(Prov. 8:6-7)

An honest witness tells the truth;
a false witness tells lies.
(Prov. 12:17)

Truthful words stand the test of time,
but lies are soon exposed.
(Prov. 12:19)

The Lord detests lying lips,
but he delights in those who tell the truth.
(Prov. 12:22)

A truthful witness saves lives,
but a false witness is a traitor.
(Prov. 14:25)

Get the truth and never sell it;
also get wisdom, discipline and good judgment.
(Prov. 23:23)

If you assist a thief,
you only hurt yourself.
You are sworn to tell the truth,
but you dare not testify.
(Prov. 29:24)

Every word of God proves true.
He is a shield
to all who come to him for protection.
(Prov. 30:5)

Those who love money
will never have enough.
How meaningless to think
that wealth brings true happiness.
(Eccles. 5:10)

# Chapter 24

# V

## VICTORY (TRIUMPH)

"You must defend my innocence, O God,
since no one else will stand up for me.
You have closed their minds to understanding,
but do not let them triumph."
(Job 17:3-4)

"Don't you realize
that from the beginning of time,
ever since people
were first placed on the earth,
the triumph of the wicked has been short-lived
and the joy of the godless
has been only temporary?"(Zophar)
(Job 20:4-5)

Victory comes from you, O Lord.
May you bless your people.
(Psalm 3:8)

You have given me your shield of victory.
Your right hand supports me;
your help has made me great.
(Psalm 18:35)

May we shout for joy
when we hear of your victory,
and raise a victory banner
in the name of our God.
May the Lord answer all your prayers.
(Psalm 20:5)

How the king rejoices in your strength, O Lord!
He shouts with joy
because you give him victory.
(Psalm 21:1)

I will exalt you, Lord,
for you rescued me.
You refused to let my enemies
triumph over me.
(Psalm 30:1)

You are my hiding place;
you protect me from trouble.
You surround me with songs of victory.
(Psalm 32:7)

They(Israel) did not conquer the land
with their swords;
it was not their own strong arm
that gave them victory.
It was your right hand and strong arm
and the blinding light from your face
that helped them, for you loved them.
You are my King and my God.
You command victories for Israel.
(Psalm 44:3-4)

Put on your sword, O mighty warrior!
You are so glorious, so majestic!
In your majesty, ride out to victory,
defending truth, humility, and justice.
Go forth to perform awe-inspiring deeds!
(Psalm 45:3-4)

As your name deserves, O God,
you will be praised to the ends of the earth.
Your strong right hand is filled with victory.
(Psalm 48:10)

I wait quietly before God,
for my victory comes from him.
He alone is my rock and my salvation,
my fortress where I will never be shaken.
(Psalm 62:1-2)

My victory and honor
come from God alone.
He is my refuge,
a rock where no enemy can reach me.
(Psalm 62:7)

Sing a new song to the Lord,
for he has done wonderful deeds
His right hand has won a mighty victory;
his holy arm has shown his saving power!
The Lord has announced his victory
and has revealed his righteousness
to every nation!
He has remembered his promise
to love and be faithful to Israel.
The ends of the earth
have seen the victory of our God.
(Psalm 98:1-3)

The Lord is for me,
so I will have no fear.
What can mere people do to me?
Yes, the Lord is for me;
he will help me.
I will look in triumph
at those who hate me.
(Psalm 118:6-7)

The Lord is my strength and my song;
he has given me victory.
Songs of joy and victory are sung
in the camp of the godly.
The strong right arm of the Lord
has done glorious things!
The strong right arm of the Lord
is raised in triumph.
(Psalm 118:14-16)

I thank you for answering my prayer
and giving me victory!
(Psalm 118:21)

For the Lord delights in his people;
he crowns the humble with victory.
Let the faithful rejoice
that he honors them.
Let them sing for joy
as they lie on their beds.
(Psalm 149:4-5)

The horse is prepared
for the day of battle,
but the victory belongs to the Lord.
(Prov. 21:31)

# Chapter 25

# W

## WEALTH (RICH)

Satan replied to the Lord,
"Yes, but Job has good reason to fear God.
You have always put a wall of protection
around him and his home and his property.
You have made him prosper
in everything he does.
Look how rich he is!
But reach out and take away everything he has,
and he will surely curse you to your face."
(Job 1:9-11)

"Even captives are at ease in death,
with no guards to curse them.
Rich and poor are both there,
and the slave is free from his master."
(Job 3:18-19)

"These wicked people
are heavy and prosperous;
their waists bulge with fat.
But their cities will be ruined.
They will live in abandoned houses
that are ready to tumble down.
Their riches will not last,
and their wealth will not endure.
Their possessions will no longer
spread across the horizon."(Eliphaz)
(Job 15: 27-29)

"Let them (wicked)
no longer fool themselves
by trusting in empty riches, for emptiness
will be their only reward."(Eliphaz)
(Job 15:31)

"They(wicked) will gie back
everything they worked for.
Their wealth will bring them no joy.
For they oppressed the poor
and left them destitute.
They foreclosed on their homes."(Zophar)
(Job 20:18-19)

"God, in his power, drags away the rich.
They may rise high,
but they have no assurance of life.
They may be allowed to live in security,
but God is always watching them."
(Job 24:22-23)

"The wicked go to bed rich
but wake to find
that all their wealth is gone.
Terror overwhelms them like a flood,
and they are blown away
in the storms of the night."
(Job 27:19-20)

"He doesn't care
how great a person may be,
and he pays no more attention
to the rich than to the poor.
He made them all."(Elihu)
(Job 34:19)

"But you are obsessed
with whether the godless will be judged.
Don't worry,
judgment and justice will be upheld.
But watch out,
or you may be seduced by wealth.
Don't let yourself
be bribed into sin.
Could all your wealth or all your mighty efforts
keep you from distress?"(Elihu)
(Job 36:17-19)

For royal power belongs to the Lord.
He rules all the nations.
Let the rich of the earth feast and worship.
Bow before him,
all who are mortal,
all whose lives will end as dust.
(Psalm 22:28-29)

It is better to be godly and have little
than to be evil and rich.
For the strength of the wicked
will be shattered,
but the Lord takes care of the godly.
(Psalm 37:16-17)

We are merely moving shadows,
and all our busy rushing
ends in nothing.
We heap up wealth,
not knowing who will spend it.
(Psalm 39:6)

So don't be dismayed
when the wicked grow rich
and their homes
become ever more splendid.
For when they die,
they take nothing with them.
Their wealth will not follow them
into the grave.
In this life they consider themselves fortunate
and are applauded for their success.
But they will die like all before them,
and never again see the light of day.
People who boast of their wealth
don't understand;
they will die, just like animals.
(Psalm 49:16-20)

Don't make your living by extortion
or put your hope in stealing.
And if your wealth increases,
don't make it the center of your life.
(Psalm 62:10)

Honor the Lord with your wealth
and with the best part
of everything you produce.
Then he will fill your barns with grain,
and your vats
will overflow with good wine.
(Prov. 3:9-10)

"I (Wisdom) love all who love me.
Those who search
will surely find me.
I have riches and honor,
as well as enduring wealth and justice.
My gifts are better than gold,
even the purest gold,
my wages better than sterling silver.
I walk in righteousness,
in paths of justice.
Those who love me inherit wealth.
I will fill their treasuries."
(Prov. 8:17-21)

Tainted wealth has no lasting value,
but right living can save your life.
(Prov. 10:2)

Lazy people are soon poor;
hard workers get rich.
(Prov. 10:4)

The wealth of the rich
is their fortress;
The poverty of the poor
is their destruction.
(Prov. 10:15)

The blessing of the Lord makes a person rich,
and he adds no sorrow with it.
(Prov. 10:22)

Riches won't help on the day of judgment,
but right living can save you from death.
(Prov. 11:4)

A gracious woman gains respect,
but ruthless men gain only wealth.
(Prov. 11:16)

Evil people get rich for the moment,
but the reward of the godly will last!
(Prov. 11:18)

Give freely and become more wealthy;
be stingy and lose everything.
(Prov. 11:24)

Some who are poor pretend to be rich;
others who are rich pretend to be poor.
(Prov. 13:7)

Wealth from get-rich-quick schemes
quickly disappears;
wealth from hard work grows over time.
(Prov. 13:11)

The poor are despised
even by their neighbors,
while the rich have many "friends."
(Prov. 14:20)

Wealth is a crown for the wise;
the effort of fools yields only foolishness.
(Prov. 14:24)

Better to have little, with godliness,
than to be rich and dishonest.
(Prov. 16:8)

The rich think of their wealth
as a strong defense;
they imagine it to be a high wall of safety.
(Prov. 18:11)

Wealth makes many "friends";
poverty drives them away.
(Prov. 19:4)

Wealth created by a lying tongue
is a vanishing mist and a deadly trap.
(Prov. 21:6)

Those who love pleasure become poor;
those who love wine and luxury
will never be rich.
(Prov. 21:17)

The wise have wealth and luxury,
but fools spend whatever they get.
(Prov. 21:20)

Choose a good reputation over great riches;
being held in high esteem
is better than silver or gold.
(Prov. 22:1)

The rich and poor have this in common:
the Lord made them both.
(Prov. 22:2)

True humility and fear of the Lord
lead to riches,honor and long life.
(Prov. 22:4)

Just as the rich rule the poor,
so the borrower is servant to the lender.
(Prov. 22:7)

A person who gets ahead
by oppressing the poor
or by showering gifts on the rich,
will end in poverty.
(Prov. 22:16)

Don't wear yourself out trying to get rich.
Be wise enough to know when to quit.
In the blink of an eye wealth disappears,
for it will sprout wings
and fly away like an eagle.
(Prov. 23:4-5)

Better to be poor and honest
than to be dishonest and rich.
(Prov. 28:6)

Rich people may think they are wise,
but a poor person with discernment
can see right through them.
(Prov. 28:11)

The trustworthy person
will get a rich reward,
but a person who wants quick riches
will get into trouble.
(Prov. 28:30)

O God, I beg two favors from you;
let me have them before I die.
First, help me never to tell a lie.
Second, give me neither poverty nor riches!
Give me just enough to satisfy my needs.
For if I grow rich,
I may deny you and say,
"Who is the Lord?"
And if I am too poor, I may steal
and thus insult God's holy name.
(Prov. 30:7-9)

I observed yet another example
of something meaningless under the sun.
This is the case of a man
who is all alone, without a child,
or a brother, yet who works hard
to gain as much wealth as he can.
But then he asks himself,
"Who am I working for?
Why am I giving up so much pleasure now?"
It is all so meaningless and depressing.
(Eccles. 4:7-8)

Those who love money will never have enough.
How meaningless to think
that wealth brings true happiness!
The more you have, the more people come
to help you spend it.
So what good is wealth—
except perhaps to watch it
slip through your fingers!
(Eccles. 5:10-11)

People who work hard sleep well,
whether they eat little or much.
But the rich
seldom get a good night's sleep.
(Eccles. 5:12)

There is another serious problem
I have seen under the sun.
Hoarding riches harms the saver.
Money is put into risky investments
that turn sour, and everything is lost.
In the end, there is nothing left to pass
on to one's children.
We all come to the end of our lives
as naked and empty-handed
as on the day we were born.
We can't take our riches with us.
(Eccles. 5:13-15)

And it is a good thing
to receive wealth from God
and the good health to enjoy it.
To enjoy your work
and accept your lot in life—
this is indeed a gift from God.
(Eccles. 5:19)

There is another serious tragedy
I have seen under the sun,
and it weighs heavily on humanity.
God gives some people great wealth and honor
and everything they could ever want,
but then he doesn't give them
the chance to enjoy these things.
They die, and someone else, even a stranger,
ends up enjoying their wealth!
This is meaningless—a sickening tragedy.
(Eccles. 6:1-2)

I have observed something else under the sun.
The fastest runner
doesn't always win the race,
and the strongest warrior
doesn't always win the battle.
The wise sometimes go hungry,
and the skillful are not necessarily wealthy.
And those who are educated
don't always lead successful lives.
It is all decided by chance,
by being in the right place at the right time.
(Eccles. 9:11)

## WICKED

"Why wasn't I buried like a stillborn child,
like a baby who never lives to see the light?
For in death the wicked cause no trouble,
and the weary are at rest."
(Job 3:16-17)

"He rescues the poor
from the cutting words of the strong,
and rescues them
from the clutches of the powerful.
And so at last the poor have hope,
and the snapping jaws
of the wicked are shut."(Eliphaz)
(Job 5:15-16)

"But look,
God will not reject a person of integrity,
nor will he lend a hand to the wicked.
He will once again
fill your mouth with laughter
and your lips with shouts of joy.
Those who hate you
will be clothed with shame,
and the home of the wicked
will be destroyed."(Bildad)
(Job 8:20-22)

"Innocent or wicked, it is all the same to God.
That's why I say,
He destroys both the blameless and the wicked
When a plague sweeps through,
he laughs at the death of the innocent.
The whole earth
is in the hands of the wicked,
and God blinds the eyes of the judges.
If he's not the one who does it, who is?
(Job 9:22:24)

"What do you gain by oppressing me?
Why do you reject me,
the work of your own hands,
while smiling on the schemes of the wicked?"
(Job 10:3)

"The wicked writhe in pain
throughout their lives.
Years of trouble
are stored up for the ruthless."(Eliphaz)
(Job 15:20)

"These wicked people are heavy and prosperous
their waists bulge with fat.
But their cities will be ruined,
they will live in abandoned houses
that are ready to tumble down.
Their riches will not last
and their wealth will not endure.
Their possessions will no longer
spread across the horizon."(Eliphaz)
(Job 15:27-29)

"People jeer and laugh at me.
They slap my cheek in contempt.
A mob gathers against me.
God has handed me over to sinners.
He has tossed me
into the hands of the wicked."
(Job 16:10-11)

"Surely the light of the wicked
will be snuffed out.
The sparks of their fire will not glow."(Bildad)
( Job 18:5)

"The confident stride of the wicked
will be shortened.
Their own schemes will be their downfall."(Bildad)
(Job 18:7)

"Don't you realize
that from the beginning of time,
ever since people
were first placed on the earth,
the triumph of the wicked
has been short lived,
and the joy of the godless
has been only temporary."(Zophar)
(Job 20:4-5)

"Why do the wicked prosper,
growing old and powerful?
They live to see their children
grow up and settle down,
and they enjoy their grandchildren.
Their homes are safe from every fear
and God does not punish them."
(Job 21:7-9)

"They(wicked) spend their days in prosperity,
then go down to the grave in peace.
And yet they say to God, Go away.
We want no part of you and your ways.
Who is the Almighty
and why should we obey him?
What good will it do us to pray?'
(They think their prosperity is of their
own doing, but I will have nothing to do
with that kind of thinking.)
Yet the light of the wicked
never seems to be extinguished.
Do they ever have trouble?
Does God distribute sorrows to them in anger?"
(Job 21:13-17)

"You will tell me
of rich and wicked people
whose houses have vanished
because of their sins.
But ask those who have been around,
and they will tell you the truth.
Evil people are spared
in times of calamity,
and are allowed to escape disaster."
(Job 21:28-30)

"Why doesn't the Almighty
bring the wicked to judgment?
Why must the godly
wait for him in vain?"
(Job 24:1)

"Wicked people rebel against the light.
They refuse to acknowledge its ways
or stay in its paths."
(Job 24:13)

"This is what the wicked will receive from God;
this is their inheritance from the Almighty.
They may have many children,
but the children will die in war
or starve to death.
Those who survive will die of a plague,
and not even their widows will mourn them."
(Job 27:13-15)

"The wicked go to bed rich
but wake to find
that all their wealth is gone."
(Job 27:19)

"For God watches how people live;
he sees everything they do.
No darkness is thick enough
to hide the wicked from his eyes."(Elihu)
(Job 34:21-22)

"Job, you deserve the maximum penalty
for the wicked way you have talked.
For you have added rebellion to your sin;
you show no respect,
and you speak
many angry words against God."(Elihu)
(Job 34:36-37)

Oh, the joys of those
who do not follow
the advice of the wicked,
or stand around with sinners
or join in with mockers.
(Psalm 1:1)

They(wicked) are like worthless chaff,
scattered by the wind.
They will be condemned
at the time of judgment.
Sinners will have no place
among the godly.
For the Lord
watches over the path of the godly,
but the path of the wicked
leads to destruction
(Psalm 1:4-6)

O God,
you take no pleasure in wickedness;
you cannot tolerate
the sins of the wicked.
Therefore the proud
may not stand in your presence,
for you hate all who do evil.
(Psalm 5:4-5)

End the evil
of those who are wicked
and defend the righteous.
For you look
deep within the mind and heart,
O righteous God.
(Psalm 7:9)

God is an honest judge.
He is angry with the wicked every day.
(Psalm 7:11)

The wicked conceive evil;
they are pregnant with trouble
and give birth to lies.
They dig a deep pit to trap others,
then fall into it themselves.
The trouble they make for others
backfires on them.
The violence they plan
falls on their own heads.
(Psalm 7:14-16)

The wicked arrogantly
hunt down the poor.
Let them be caught
in the evil they plan for others.
For they brag
about their evil desires;
they praise the greedy and curse the Lord.
The wicked are too proud to seek God.
They seem to think that God is dead.
Yet they succeed
in everything they do.
They do not see
your punishment awaiting them.
They sneer at all their enemies.
They think,
"Nothing bad will ever happen to us!
We will be free of trouble forever!"
(Psalm 10:2-6)

The wicked think,
"God isn't watching us!
He has closed his eyes
and won't even see what we do!"
(Psalm 10:11)

Why do the wicked
get away with despising God?
They think,
"God will never call us to account."
But you see the trouble
and grief they cause.
You take note of it and punish them.
The helpless put their trust in you.
You defend the orphans.
(Psalm 10:13-14)

But the Lord is in his holy Temple;
the Lord still rules from heaven.
He watches everyone closely,
examining every person on earth.
The Lord examines
both the righteous and the wicked.
He hates those who love violence.
(Psalm 11:4-5)

The wicked frustrate
the plans of the oppressed,
but the Lord will protect his people.
(Psalm 14:6)

To the pure
you show yourself pure,
but to the wicked
you show yourself hostile.
(Psalm 18:26)

Many sorrows come to the wicked,
but unfailing love
surrounds those who trust the Lord.
(Psalm 32:10)

Calamity will surely
overtake the wicked,
and those who hate the righteous
will be punished.
(Psalm 34:21)

Sin whispers to the wicked,
deep within their hearts.
They have no fear of God at all.
In their blind conceit,
they cannot see
how wicked they really are.
(Psalm 36:1-2)

Don't worry about the wicked
or envy those who do wrong.
For like grass,
they soon fade away.
Like spring flowers, they soon wither.
(Psalm 37:1-2)

Stop being angry!
Turn from your rage!
Do not lose your temper—
it only leads to harm.
For the wicked will be destroyed,
but those who trust in the Lord
will possess the land.
Soon the wicked will disappear.
Though you look for them,
they will be gone.
(Psalm 37:8-10)

The wicked borrow and never repay,
but the godly are generous givers.
(Psalm 37:21)

I have seen wicked and ruthless people
flourishing like a tree
in its native soil.
But when I looked again,
they were gone!
Though I searched for them,
I could not find them.
(Psalm 37:35-36)

So don't be dismayed
when the wicked grow rich
and their homes become ever more splendid.
For when they die,
they take nothing with them.
Their wealth will not follow them
into the grave.
In this life
they consider themselves fortunate
and are applauded for their success.
But they will die
like all before them
and never again see the light of day.
(Psalm 49:16-19)

My God,
rescue me from the power of the wicked,
from the clutches of cruel oppressors.
(Psalm 71:4)

Look at these wicked people—
enjoying a life of ease
while their riches multiply.
Did I keep my heart pure for nothing?
Did I keep myself innocent for no reason?
I get nothing but trouble all day long;
every morning brings me pain.
(Psalm 73:12-14)

Though the wicked sprout like weeds
and evildoers flourish,
they will be destroyed forever.
But you, O Lord,
will be exalted forever.
(Psalm 92:7-8)

How long, O Lord?
How long will the wicked
be allowed to gloat?
How long will they speak with arrogance?
How long will these evil people boast?
(Psalm 94:3-4)

The wicked have set their traps for me,
but I will not turn
from your commandments.
(Psalm 119:110)

The Lord supports the humble,
but he brings the wicked
down into the dust.
(Psalm 147:6)

Don't envy violent people
or copy their ways.
Such wicked people
are detestable to the Lord,
but he offers his friendship
to the godly.
The Lord curses the house of the wicked,
but he blesses the home of the upright!
(Prov. 3:31-33)

The way of the righteous
is like the first gleam of dawn,
which shines ever brighter
until the full light of day.
But the way of the wicked
is like total darkness.
They have no idea
what they are stumbling over.
(Prov. 4:18-19)

What are worthless and wicked people like?
They are constant liars.
(Prov. 6:12)

Anyone who rebukes a mocker
will get an insult in return.
Anyone who corrects the wicked
will get hurt.
(Prov. 9:7)

We have happy memories of the godly,
but the name of a wicked person rots away.
(Prov. 10:7)

The words of the godly
are a life-giving fountain;
the words of the wicked
conceal violent intentions.
(Prov. 10:11)

The fears of the wicked will be fulfilled;
the hopes of the godly will be granted.
(Prov. 10:24)

When the storms of life come
the wicked are whirled away,
but the godly
have a lasting foundation.
(Prov. 10:25)

Fear of the Lord
lengthens one's life,
but the years of the wicked are cut short.
(Prov. 10:27)

The hope of the godly
result in happiness.
but the expectations of the wicked
come to nothing.
(Prov. 10:28)

The way of the Lord
is a stronghold to those with integrity.
but it destroys the wicked.
(Prov. 10:29)

The lips of the godly
speak helpful words,
but the mouth of the wicked
speak perverse words.
(Prov. 10:32)

The godly are directed by honesty;
the wicked fall beneath their load of sin.
(Prov. 11:5)

When the wicked die,
their hopes die with them,
for they rely on their own feeble strength.
(Prov. 11:7)

Upright citizens are good for a city
and make it prosper,
but the talk of the wicked
tears it apart.
(Prov. 11:11)

The godly can look forward to a reward,
while the wicked can expect only judgment.
(Prov. 11:23)

The plans of the godly are just;
the advice of the wicked is treacherous.
(Prov. 12:5)

The words of the wicked
are like a murderous ambush,
but the words of the godly saves lives.
(Prov. 12:6)

The godly care for their animals,
but the wicked are always cruel.
(Prov. 12:10)

The wicked are trapped
by their own words,
but the godly escape such trouble.
(Prov. 12:13)

The godly give good advice
to their friends,
the wicked lead them astray.
(Prov. 12:26)

The godly hate lies
the wicked cause shame and disgrace,
(Prov. 13:5)

The life of the godly
is full of light and joy,
but the light of the wicked
will be snuffed out.
(Prov. 13:9)

The house of the wicked will be destroyed,
but the tent of the godly will flourish.
(Prov. 14:11)

There is treasure in the house of the godly,
but the earnings of the wicked bring trouble.
(Prov. 15:6)

The Lord detests the sacrifice of the wicked,
but he delights in the prayers of the upright
(Prov. 15:8)

The Lord detests the way of the wicked,
but he loves those who pursue godliness.
(Prov. 15:9)

The Lord has made everything
for his own purposes,
even the wicked for a day of disaster.
(Prov. 16:4)

The wicked take secret bribes
to pervert the course of justice.
(Prov. 17:23)

A corrupt witness
makes a mockery of justice;
the mouth of the wicked gulps down evil.
(Prov. 19:28)

The violence of the wicked
sweeps them away,
because they refuse to do what is just.
(Prov. 21:7)

The wicked bluff their way through,
but the virtuous think before they act.
(Prov. 21:29)

The godly may trip seven times,
but they will get up again.
But one disaster
is enough to overthrow the wicked.
(Prov. 24:16)

Don't fret because of evildoers;
don't envy the wicked.
For evil people have no future;
the light of the wicked
will be snuffed out.
(Prov. 24:19-20)

If the godly give in to the wicked,
it's like polluting a fountain
or muddying a spring.
(Prov. 25:26)

The wicked run away
when no one is chasing them,
but the godly are as bold as lions.
(Prov. 28:1)

When the godly succeed,
everyone is glad.
When the wicked take charge,
people go into hiding.
(Prov. 28:12)

A wicked ruler
is as dangerous to the poor
as a roaring lion or an attacking bear.
(Prov. 28:15)

When the godly are in authority,
the people rejoice.
But when the wicked are in power,
they groan.
(Prov. 29:2 )

When the wicked are in authority,
sin flourishes,
but the godly will live to see their downfall.
(Prov. 29:16)

I have seen everything
in this meaningless life
including the death of good young people,
and the long life of wicked people.
So don't be too good or too wise!
Why destroy yourself?
On the other hand,
don't be too wicked either.
Don't be a fool!
Why die before your time?
Pay attention to these instructions,
for anyone who fears God will avoid both extremes.
(Eccles. 7:15-18)

None of us can hold back
our spirit from departing.
None of us has the power
to prevent the day of our death.
There is no escaping that obligation,
that dark battle.
And in the face of death,
wickedness will certainly not rescue the wicked.
(Eccles. 8:8)

I have seen wicked people
buried with honor.
Yet they were the very ones
who frequented the Temple
and are now praised in the same city
where they committed their crimes!
(Eccles. 8:10)

The wicked will not prosper,
for they do not fear God.
Their days will never grow long
like the evening shadows.
And this is not all
that is meaningless in our world.
In this life,
good people are often treated
as though they were wicked,
and wicked people are often treated
as though they were good.
This is meaningless!
(Eccles. 8:13-14)

The same destiny
ultimately awaits everyone,
whether righteous or wicked, good or bad,
ceremonially clean or unclean,
religious or irreligious.
Good people receive the same treatment
as sinners,
and people who make promises to God
are treated like people who don't.
(Eccles. 9:2)

## WIFE

Drink water from your own well—
share your love only with your wife.
Why spill the water of your springs
in the streets, having sex with just anyone?
You should reserve it for yourselves.
Never share it with strangers.
Let your wife
be a fountain of blessing for you.
Rejoice in the wife of your youth.
She is a loving deer, a graceful doe.
Let her breasts satisfy you always.
May you always be captivated by her love.
Why be captivated, my son,
by an immoral woman,
or fondle the breasts of a promiscuous woman?
(Prov. 5:15-20)

The man who finds a wife
finds a treasure,
and he receives favor from the Lord.
(Prov. 18:22)

A quarrelsome wife is as annoying
as constant dripping.
(Prov. 19:13)

It's better to live alone
in the corner of the attic
than with a quarrelsome wife in a lovely home.
(Prov. 21:9)

It is better to live alone in the desert
than with a quarrelsome, complaining wife.
(Prov. 21:19)

Who can find a virtuous and capable wife?
She is more precious than rubies.
Her husband can trust her,
and she will greatly enrich his life.
She brings him good, not harm,
all the days of her life.
She finds wool and flax and busily spins it.
She is like a merchant ship,
bringing her food from afar.
She gets up before dawn
to prepare breakfast for her household,
and plan the day's work for her servant girls.
She goes to inspect a field and buys it;
with her earnings she plants a vineyard.
She is energetic and strong, a hard worker.
She makes sure her dealings are profitable;
her lamp burns late into the night.
Her hands are busy spinning thread,
her fingers twisting fiber.
She extends a helping hand to the poor
and opens her arms to the needy.
She has no fear of winter for her household,
for everyone has warm clothes.
She makes her own bedspreads.
She dresses in fine linen and purple gowns.

Her husband is well known at the city gates,
where he sits with the other civic leaders.
She makes belted linen garments and sashes
to sell to the merchants.
She is clothed with strength and dignity.
and she laughs without fear of the future.
When she speaks, her words are wise,
and she gives instructions with kindness.
She carefully watches everything
in her household,
and suffers nothing to laziness.
Her children stand and bless her.
Her husband praises her:
"There are many virtuous and capable women
in the world,
but you surpass them all!"
(Prov. 31:10-29)

## WISDOM (WISE)

"He(God) frustrates the plans of schemers
so the work of their hands will not succeed.
He traps the wise in their own cleverness
so their cunning schemes are thwarted."(Eliphaz)
(Job 5:12-13)

"Just ask the previous generation.
Pay attention to the experience of our ancestors.
For we were born but yesterday and know nothing.
Our days on earth are as fleeting as a shadow.
But those who came before us will teach you.
They will teach you the wisdom of old."(Bildad)
(Job 8:8-10)

"If someone wanted to take God to court,
would it be possible to nswer him
even once in a thousand times?
For God is so wise and so mighty.
Who has ever challenged him successfully?"
(Job 9:3-4)

"If only God would speak;
if only he would tell you what he thinks!
If only he would tell you
the secrets of wisdom,
for true wisdom is not a simple matter.
Listen!
God is doubtless punishing you
far less than you deserve!"(Zophar)
(Job 11:5-6)

"You people really know everything, don't you?
And when you die,
wisdom will die with you!
Well, I know a few things myself—
and you're no better than I am.
Who doesn't know these things
you've been saying?"
(Job 12:2-3)

"Wisdom belongs to the aged,
and understanding to the old.
But true wisdom and power are found in God;
counsel and understanding are his."
(Job 12:12-13)

"Yes, strength and wisdom are his;
deceivers and deceived
are both in his power.
He leads counselors away,
stripped of good judgment;
wise judges become fools."
(Job 12:16-17)

"As for you, you smear me with lies.
As physicians, you are worthless quacks.
If only you could be silent!
That's the wisest thing you could do."
(Job 13:4-5)

"A wise man wouldn't answer
with such empty talk!
You are nothing but a windbag.
The wise don't engage in empty chatter.
What good are such words?"(Eliphaz)
(Job 15:2-3)

"Were you listening at God's secret council?
Do you have a monopoly on wisdom?
What do you know that we don't?
What do you understand
that we do not?"(Eliphaz)
(Job 15:8-9)

"Can a person do anything to help God?
Can even a wise person
be helpful to him?"(Eliphaz)
(Job 22:2)

"But do people know
where to find wisdom?
Where can they find understanding?
No one knows where to find it,
for it is not found among the living."
(Job 28:12-13)

"Wisdom is more valuable
than gold and crystal.
It cannot be purchased
with jewels mounted in fine gold.
Coral and jasper are worthless
in trying to get it.
The price of wisdom is far above rubies."
(Job 28:17-18)

"God alone understands the way to wisdom;
he knows where it can be found,
for he looks
throughout the whole earth
and sees everything under the heavens.
He decided how hard the winds should blow
and how much rain should fall.
He made the laws for the rain
and laid out a path for the lightning.
Then he saw wisdom and evaluated it.
He set it in place
and examined it thoroughly.
And this is what he says to all humanity:
'The fear of the Lord is true wisdom;
to forsake evil is real understanding.'"
(Job 28:23-28)

"I am young and you are old,
so I held back from telling you what I think.
I thought,
'Those who are older should speak,
for wisdom comes with age.'
But there is a spirit within people,
the breath of the Almighty within them,
that makes them intelligent.
Sometimes the elders are not wise.
Sometimes the aged
do not understand justice."(Elihu)
(Job 32:6-9)

"We cannot imagine
the power of the Almighty;
but even though he is just and righteous
he does not destroy us.
No wonder people everywhere fear him.
All who are wise
show him reverence."(Elihu)
(Job 37:23-24)

Then the Lord answered Job
from the whirlwind:
"Who is this that questions my wisdom
with such ignorant words?
Brace yourself like a man,
because I have some questions for you,
and you must answer them."
(Job 38:1-3)

(God questions Job)
"Can you shout to the clouds and make it rain?
Can you make lightning appear
and cause it to strike as you direct?
Who gives intuition to the heart
and instinct to the mind?
Who is wise enough to count all the clouds?
Who can tilt the water jars of heaven
when the parched ground is dry
and the soil has hardened into clods?"
(Job 38:34-38)

"The ostrich flaps her wings grandly,
but they are no match
for the feathers of the stork.
She lays her eggs on top of the earth,
letting them be warmed in the dust.
She doesn't worry
that a foot might crush them
or a wild animal might destroy them.
She is harsh toward her young,
as if they were not her own.
She doesn't care if they die.
For God has deprived her of wisdom.
He has given her no understanding.
But whenever she jumps up to run,
she passes the swiftest horse with its rider."
(Job 39:13-18)

"Is it your wisdom that makes the hawk soar
and spread its wings toward the south?
Is it at your command that the eagle rises
to the heights to make its nest?
It lives on the cliffs,
making its home on a distant, rocky crag."
(Job 39:26-28)

Then Job replied to the Lord:
"I know that you can do anything,
and no one can stop you.
You asked,
'Who is this that questions my wisdom
with such ignorance?'
It is I—and I was talking about things
I knew nothing about,
things far too wonderful for me."
(Job 42:1-3)

The Lord looks down from heaven
on the entire human race;
he looks to see if anyone is truly wise,
if anyone seeks God.
But no, all have turned away;
all have become corrupt.
No one does good, not a single one!
(Psalm 14:2-3)

The instructions of the Lord are perfect,
reviving the soul.
The decrees of the Lord are trustworthy,
making wise the simple.
(Psalm 19:7)

Listen to this, all you people!
Pay attention, everyone in the world!
High and low, rich and poor—listen!
For my words are wise,
and my thoughts are filled with insight.
I listen carefully to many proverbs
and solve riddles
with inspiration from a harp.
(Psalm 49:1-4)

Those who are wise must finally die,
just like the foolish and the senseless,
leaving all their wealth behind.
(Psalm 49:10)

For I was born a sinner—
yes, from the moment my mother conceived me.
But you desire honesty from the womb,
teaching me wisdom even there.
(Psalm 51:5-6)

Teach us to realize the brevity of life,
so that we may grow in wisdom.
(Psalm 90:12)

Those who are wise
will take all this to heart;
they will see in our history
the faithful love of the Lord.
(Psalm 107:43)

Fear of the Lord
is the foundation of true wisdom.
All who obey his commandments
will grow in wisdom.
(Psalm 111:10)

Oh, how I love your instructions!
I think about them all day long.
Your commands make me
wiser than my enemies,
for they are my constant guide.
Yes, I have more insight than my teachers,
for I am always thinking of your laws.
I am even wiser than my elders,
for I have kept your commandments.
(Psalm 119:97-100)

Fear of the Lord
is the foundation of true knowledge,
but fools despise wisdom and discipline.
(Prov. 1:7)

Wisdom shouts in the streets.
She cries out in the public square.
She calls to the crowds
along the main street,
to those gathered in front of the city gate:
"How long, you simpletons,
will you insist on being simpleminded?
How long will you mockers
relish your mocking?
How long will you fools hate knowledge?
Come and listen to my counsel.
I'll share my heart with you
and make you wise."
(Prov. 1:20-23)

My child, listen to what I say,
and treasure my commands.
Tune your ears to wisdom,
and concentrate on understanding.
Cry out for insight,
and ask for understanding.
Search for them as you would for silver;
seek them like hidden treasures.
Then you will understand
what it means to fear the Lord,
and you will gain knowledge of God.
For the Lord grants wisdom!
From his mouth
come knowledge and understanding.
(Prov. 2:1-6)

Wisdom will save you from evil people,
from those whose words are twisted.
These men turn from the right way
to walk down dark paths.
They take pleasure in doing wrong,
and they enjoy the twisted ways of evil.
Their actions are crooked,
and their ways are wrong.
(Prov. 2:12-15)

Wisdom will save you
from the immoral woman,
from the seductive words
of the promiscuous woman.
(Prov. 2:16)

Don't be impressed with your own wisdom
Instead, fear the Lord
and turn away from evil.
(Prov. 3:7)

Joyful is the person who finds wisdom,
the one who gains understanding.
For wisdom is more profitable than silver,
and her wages are better than gold.
Wisdom is more precious than rubies;
nothing you desire
can compare with her.
She offers you long life
in her right hand,
and riches and honor in her left.
She will guide you
down delightful paths;
all her ways are satisfying.
Wisdom is a tree of life
to those who embrace her;
happy are those who hold her tightly.
(Prov. 3:13-18)

By wisdom the Lord founded the earth;
by understanding he created the heavens.
(Prov. 3:19)

The wise inherit honor,
but fools are put to shame.
(Prov. 3:35)

Don't turn your back on wisdom,
for she will protect you.
Love her and she will guard you.
Getting wisdom
is the wisest thing you can do!
And whatever else you do,
develop good judgment.
If you prize wisdom,
she will make you great.
Embrace her, and she will honor you.
(Prov. 4:6-8)

Take a lesson from the ants,
you lazybones.
Learn from their ways and become wise!
Though they have no prince
or governor or ruler to make them work,
they labor hard all summer,
gathering food for the winter.
(Prov. 6:6-8)

Love wisdom like a sister,
make insight
a beloved member of your family.
(Prov. 7:4)

For wisdom is far more valuable than rubies.
Nothing you desire can compare with it.
(Prov. 8:11)

"I, Wisdom live together with good judgment.
I know where to discover
knowledge and discernment."
(Prov. 8:12)

"All who fear the Lord will hate evil.
Therefore, I hate pride and arrogance,
corruption and perverse speech.
Common sense and success belong to me.
Insight and strength are mine."
(Prov. 8:13-14)

"Because of me, kings reign,
and rulers make just decrees.
Rulers lead with my help,
and nobles make righteous judgments."
(Prov. 8:15-16)

"I love all who love me.
Those who search will surely find me.
I have riches and honor,
as well as enduring wealth and justice.
My gifts are better than gold,
even the purest gold,
my wages better than sterling silver!
I walk in righteousness,
in paths of justice.
Those who love me inherit wealth.
I will fill their treasuries."
(Prov. 8:17-21)

"The Lord formed me from the beginning,
before he created anything else.
I was appointed in ages past,
at the very first, before the earth began.
I was born before the oceans were created,
before the springs bubbled forth their waters.
Before the mountains were formed,
before the hills, I was born—
before he had made the earth and the fields
and the first handfulls of soil.
I was there when he established the heavens,
when he drew the horizon on the oceans.
I was there when he set the clouds above,
when he established springs deep in the earth.
I was there when he set the limits of the seas,
so they would not spread beyond their boundaries.
And when he marked off the earth's foundations,
I was the architect at his side.
I was his constant delight,
rejoicing always in his presence.
And how happy I was with the world he created;
how I rejoiced with the human family!"
(Prov. 8:22-31)

"And so, my children, listen to me,
for all who follow my ways are joyful.
Listen to my instruction and be wise.
Don't ignore it.
Joyful are those who listen to me,
watching for me daily at my gates,
waiting for me outside my home!
For whoever finds me finds life
and receives favor from the Lord.
But those who miss me injure themselves.
All who hate me love death."
(Prov. 8:32-36)

Instruct the wise
and they will be even wiser.
Teach the righteous
and they will learn even more.
(Prov. 9:9)

Fear of the Lord is the foundation of wisdom.
Knowledge of the Holy One
results in good judgment.
(Prov. 9:10)

Wisdom will multiply your days
and add years to your life.
(Prov. 9:11)

If you become wise
you will be the one to benefit.
If you scorn wisdom
you will be the one to suffer.
(Prov. 9:12)

A wise child brings joy to a father;
a foolish child brings grief to a mother.
(Prov. 10:1)

Wise people treasure knowledge,
but the babbling of a fool invites disaster.
(Prov. 10:14)

Pride leads to disgrace,
but with humility comes wisdom.
(Prov. 11:2)

Without wise leadership,
a nation falls;
there is safety in having many advisers.
(Prov. 11:14)

Those who bring trouble on their families
inherit the wind.
The fool will be a servant to the wise.
(Prov. 11:29)

The seeds of good deeds
become a tree of life.
a wise person wins friends.
(Prov. 11:30)

Wise words bring many benefits,
and hard work brings rewards.
(Prov. 12:14)

Fools think their own way is right,
but the wise listen to others.
(Prov. 12:15)

A fool is quick-tempered,
but a wise person stays calm when insulted.
(Prov. 12:16)

The wise don't make a show of their knowledge,
but fools broadcast their foolishness.
(Prov. 12:23)

A wise child accepts a parent's discipline;
a mocker refuses to listen to correction.
(Prov. 13:1)

Pride leads to conflict;
those who take advice are wise.
(Prov. 13:10)

The instruction of the wise
is like a life-giving fountain;
Those who accept it avoid the snares of death.
(Prov. 13:14)

Wise people think before they act;
fools don't—
and even brag about their foolishness.
(Prov.13:16)

Walk with the wise and become wise;
associate with fools and get in trouble.
(Prov. 13:20)

A fool's proud talk
becomes a rod that beats him,
but the words of the wise keep them safe.
(Prov. 14:3)

The wise are cautious and avoid danger;
fools plunge ahead with reckless confidence.
(Prov. 14:16)

Wisdom is enshrined in an understanding heart;
wisdom is not found among fools.
(Prov.14:33)

The tongue of the wise
makes knowledge appealing,
but the mouth of a fool belches out foolishness.
(Prov. 15:2)

Only a fool despises a parent's discipline;
whoever learns from correction is wise.
(Prov. 15:5)

The lips of the wise give good advice;
the heart of a fool has none to give.
(Prov. 15:7)

A wise person is hungry for knowledge,
while the fool feeds on trash.
(Prov. 15:14)

The path of life leads upward for the wise;
they leave the grave behind.
(Prov. 15:24)

If you listen to constructive criticism,
you will be at home among the wise.
(Prov. 15:31)

Fear of the Lord teaches wisdom;
humility precedes honor.
(Prov. 15:33)

How much better to get wisdom than gold,
and good judgment than silver.
(Prov. 16:16)

The wise are known for their understanding,
and pleasant words are persuasive.
(Prov. 16:21)

From a wise mind comes wise speech;
the words of the wise are persuasive.
(Prov. 16:23)

A truly wise person uses few words;
a person with understanding is even-tempered.
(Prov. 17:27)

Even fools are thought wise
when they keep silent;
with their mouths shut, they seem intelligent.
(Prov. 17:28)

Wise words are like deep waters,
wisdom flows from the wise
like a bubbling brook.
(Prov. 18:4)

Wise words satisfy like a good meal;
the right words bring satisfaction.
(Prov. 18:20)

To acquire wisdom is to love oneself;
people who cherish understanding will prosper.
(Prov. 19:8)

Get all the advice and instruction you can,
so you will be wise the rest of your life.
(Prov.19:20)

Wine produces mockers;
alcohol leads to brawls.
Those led astray by drink cannot be wise.
(Prov. 20:1)

Wise words are more valuable
than much gold and many rubies.
(Prov. 20:15)

The wise have wealth and luxury,
but fools spend whatever they get.
(Prov. 21:20)

No human wisdom or understanding or plan
can stand against the Lord.
(Prov. 21:30)

Don't wear yourself out trying to get rich.
be wise enough to know when to quit.
(Prov. 23:4)

Get the truth and never sell it;
also get wisdom, discipline and good judgment.
(Prov. 23:23)

The wise are mightier than the strong,
and those with knowledge grow stronger and stronger.
(Prov. 24:5)

Here are some further sayings of the wise:
It is wrong to show favoritism
when passing judgment.
A judge who says to the wicked, "You are innocent"
will be cursed by many people
and denounced by the nations.
But it will go well for those
who convict the guilty;
rich blessings will be showered on them.
(Prov. 24:23-25)

Be sure to answer the foolish arguments of fools,
or they will become wise in their own estimation.
(Prov. 26:5)

When there is a moral rot within a nation,
it's government topples easily.
But wise and knowledgeable leaders bring stability.
(Prov. 28:2)

Young people who obey the law are wise;
those with wild friends
bring shame to their parents.
(Prov. 28:7)

Rich people may think they are wise,
but a poor person with discernment
can see right through them.
(Prov. 28:11)

Those who trust their own insight are foolish,
but anyone who walks in wisdom is safe.
(Prov. 28:26)

Fools vent their anger,
but the wise quietly hold it back.
(Prov. 29:11)

I, the Teacher, was king of Israel,
and I lived in Jerusalem.
I devoted myself to search for understanding
and to explore by wisdom
everything being done under heaven.
I soon discovered that God has dealt
a tragic existence to the human race.
I observed everything going on under the sun,
and really, it is all meaningless—
like chasing the wind.
(Eccles. 1:12-14)

The greater my wisdom, the greater my grief.
To increase knowledge only increases sorrow.
(Eccles. 1:18)

I thought, "Wisdom is better than foolishness,
just as light is better than darkness.
For the wise can see where they are going,
but fools walk in the dark."
Yet I saw that the wise and the foolish
share the same fate. Both will die.
So I said to myself,
"Since I will end up the same as the fool,
what's the value of all my wisdom?
This is all so meaningless!"
For the wise and the foolish both die.
The wise will not be remembered
any longer than the fool.
In the days to come, both will be forgotten.
(Eccles. 2:13-16)

God gives wisdom, knowledge and joy
to those who please him.
But if a sinner becomes wealthy,
God takes the wealth away
and gives it to those who please him.
This too is meaningless—like chasing the wind.
(Eccles. 2:26)

A wise person thinks a lot about death,
while a fool thinks only about having a good time.
(Eccles. 7:4)

Better to be criticized by a wise person
than to be praised by a fool.
(Eccles. 7:5)

Extortion turns wise people into fools,
and bribes corrupt the heart.
(Eccles. 7:7)

Don't long for "the good old days."
This is not wise.
(Eccles.7:10)

Wisdom is even better when you have money.
Both are a benefit as you through life.
Wisdom and money
can get you almost anything,
but only wisdom can save your life.
(Eccles. 7:11-12)

I have always tried my best
to let wisdom guide my thoughts and actions.
I said to myself,
"I am determined to be wise."
But it didn't work.
Wisdom is always distant and difficult to find.
(Eccles. 7:23-24)

How wonderful to be wise,
to analyze and interpret things.
Wisdom lights up a person's face,
softening its harshness.
(Eccles. 8:1)

In my search for wisdom,
and in my observation
of people's burdens here on earth,
I discovered that there is ceaseless activity,
day and night.
I realized that no one can discover
everything God is doing under the sun.
Not even the wisest people discover everything,
no matter what they claim.
( Eccles. 8:16-18)

This too I carefully explored:
Even though the actions of godly people
and wise people are in God's hands,
no one knows
whether God will show them favor.
(Eccles. 9:1)

I have observed something else under the sun.
The fastest runner doesn't always win the race,
and the strongest warrior
doesn't always win the battle.
The wise sometimes go hungry,
and the skillful are not necessarily wealthy.
And those who are educated
don't always lead successful lives.
It is all decided by chance,
by being in the right place at the right time.
(Eccles. 9:11)

Better to hear the quiet words
of a wise person
than the shouts of a foolish king.
Better to have wisdom
than weapons of war,
but one sinner can destroy much that is good.
(Eccles. 9:17-18)

A wise person chooses the right road;
a fool takes the wrong one.
(Eccles. 10:2)

Using a dull ax requires great strength,
so sharpen the blade.
That's the value of wisdom;
it helps you succeed.
(Eccles. 10:10)

Wise words bring approval,
but fools are destroyed
by their own words.
(Eccles.10:12)

## WORK

Work brings profit,
but mere talk leads to poverty!
(Prov. 14:23)

Good planning and hard work
lead to prosperity,
but hasty short cuts lead to poverty.
(Prov. 21:5)

But as I looked at everything
I had worked so hard to accomplish,
it was all so meaningless—like chasing the wind.
There was nothing really worthwhile anywhere.
(Eccles. 2:11)

So I came to hate life
because everything done here under the sun
is so troubling.
Everything is meaningless—like chasing the wind.
I came to hate all my hard work here on earth,
for I must leave to others
everything I have earned.
And who can tell
whether my successors will be wise or foolish?
Yet they will control
everything I have gained by my skill
and hard work under the sun.
How meaningless!
So I gave up in despair, questioning the value
of all my hard work in this world.
Some people work wisely with knowledge and skill,
then must leave the fruit of their efforts
to someone who hasn't worked for it.

This too is meaningless, a great tragedy.
So what do people get in this life
for all their hard work and anxiety?
Their days of labor are filled with pain and grief:
even at night their minds cannot rest.
It is all meaningless.
So I decided there is nothing better
than to enjoy food and drink
and to find satisfaction in work.
Then I realized that these pleasures
are from the hand of God
For who can eat or enjoy anything apart from him?
(Eccles. 2:17-25)

People who work hard sleep well,
whether they eat little or much.
But the rich seldom get a good night's sleep.
(Eccles.5:12)

# Chapter 26

## YOUNG (YOUTH)

The glory of the young is their strength;
the gray hair of experience is the splendor of the old.
(Prov. 20:29)

Young people who obey the law are wise;
those with wild friends bring shame to their parents.
(Prov. 28:7)

Young people, it's wonderful to be young!
Enjoy every minute of it.
Do everything you want to do;
take it all in.
But remember that you must give
an account to God for everything you do.
(Eccles. 11:9)

Don't let the excitement of youth
cause you to forget your Creator.
Honor him in your youth
before you grow old and say,
"Life is not pleasant anymore."
(Eccles. 12:1)